REFORMING
SECONDARY SCIENCE INSTRUCTION

REFORMING
SECONDARY SCIENCE INSTRUCTION

Edited by Julie Gess-Newsome, Julie A. Luft, and Randy L. Bell

National Science Teachers Association

Claire Reinburg, Director
Jennifer Horak, Managing Editor
Judy Cusick, Senior Editor
J. Andrew Cocke, Associate Editor
Betty Smith, Associate Editor

ART AND DESIGN, Will Thomas, Jr., Director
Tracey Shipley, Cover and Book Design

PRINTING AND PRODUCTION, Catherine Lorrain, Director

NATIONAL SCIENCE TEACHERS ASSOCIATION
Francis Q. Eberle, PhD, Executive Director
David Beacom, Publisher

LIBRARY OF CONGRESS CATALOGING-IN-PUBLICATION DATA
Reforming secondary science instruction / edited by Julie Gess-Newsome, Julie A. Luft, and Randy L. Bell.
    p. cm.
  Includes bibliographical references and index.
  ISBN 978-1-935155-03-4
  1. Science--Study and teaching (Secondary)--United States. 2. Inquiry-based learning--United States. 3.
Educational technology--Study and teaching (Secondary)--United States. I. Gess-Newsome, Julie. II. Luft,
Julie. III. Bell, Randy L.
  Q183.3.A1R446 2008
  507.1'273--dc22
                                    2008035065

CONTENTS

Preface

Reforming Secondary Science Instruction and its companion volumes, *Technology in the Secondary Science Classroom* and *Science as Inquiry in the Secondary Setting* (both available from the National Science Teachers Association [NSTA]), have a long and interesting history. The ideas for these books emerged from our work with secondary science teachers, supportive program officers at the National Science Foundation, and the science education community, which is always seeking a connection of theory and practice. To ensure that these books were connected to each of these stakeholders, we adopted a writing plan that involved representatives from all three groups. We considered novel approaches to identify and support science teachers and science educators to participate in the project, and we sought guidance from program officers about the format and dissemination of the final product.

To begin with, we identified three topics of interest to both science teachers and science educators—science as inquiry, educational technology, and science education reform. We wanted the community of science educators to help define the content of each book, so we solicited chapter proposals from science teachers and science teacher educators. The response was impressive, with more than 50 chapter proposals submitted for the three books. Our selection of the chapters was based on the clarity of the topic, the type of idea presented, and the importance of the topic to science teachers.

Chapter authors were then asked to generate a first draft. These chapters were shared among the authors of their respective books for review. We met as a group at the annual meeting of the Association of Science Teacher Educators, in Portland, Oregon, to discuss and provide feedback to one another on our chapters. This session was extremely useful, and several of the authors returned to their chapters, ready for another revision.

Once the second revision was complete, we wanted to draw on the expertise of science teachers, whom we felt should ground this work. We contacted NSTA and placed a "call for reviewers" in their weekly electronic newsletter. More than 200 teachers offered to review our chapters. Reviews were shared with the chapter authors.

The second revision was also shared among the authors within each book. Each author now had external reviews from teachers, as well as reviews from other authors. To discuss these reviews and the final revision of the chapters, we met one more time at the annual meeting of the National Association for Research in Science Teaching, in San Francisco, California. At the conclusion of this meeting, chapter authors were ready to write their final versions.

When the chapters were completed and the books were in a publishable format, we approached NSTA about publishing them both in print and online, so that they would reach as many teachers as possible. NSTA has historically offered one chapter per book for free, but the editors at NSTA felt the time was right to attempt to offer all the chapters of these three books for free online for teachers. By doing so, we are breaking new ground in publishing. Of course, paper copies of each book are available for purchase, for those who prefer print versions. We also asked, and NSTA agreed, that any royalties from the books would go to NSTA's teacher scholarship fund to enable teachers to attend NSTA conferences.

This process has indeed been interesting, and we would like to formally thank the people who have been helpful in the development and dissemination of these books. We thank Carole Stearns for believing in this project; Mike Haney for his ongoing support; Patricia Morrell for helping to arrange meeting rooms for our chapter reviews; the 100-plus teachers who wrote reviews on the chapters; Claire Reinburg, Judy Cusick, and Andrew Cocke of NSTA for their work on these books; Lynn Bell for her technical edits of all three books; and the staff at NSTA for agreeing to pilot this book in a downloadable format so it is free to any science teacher.

—*Julie Gess-Newsome, Julie A. Luft, and Randy L. Bell*

INTRODUCTION TO SCIENCE EDUCATION REFORM

1

Change in Secondary Science Settings: A Voice From the Field

Lee Meadows
University of Alabama at Birmingham

Picture life when you are 75 years old. Your teaching career is over and you've been retired for about 10 years. You now depend on your former students to take care of you. Your former students are your doctors and nurses, bank managers and tellers, legislators and policy makers, and the brokers and analysts who manage your retirement funds. They keep food on your table, take care of your housing repairs and improvements, and run your utilities. As you think about being dependent on today's students one day, are you concerned? Most teachers are. They don't see today's students as having the skill sets necessary to maintain America's economy.

Science education reforms were instituted to address these concerns and change students' school experiences to prepare them for life and work in today's global economy (NCEE 1983). Learning science by inquiry is central to these reforms. In today's working world, students need skills for finding, organizing, and managing information. They also need rich skills for working with others and for communicating orally and in print. To maintain this country's leadership amidst fierce global competition (see Friedman 2005), students will need to be tough-minded and goal-oriented, and they will need to value their work. Inquiry helps students develop all of these skills. The secondary science reforms are focused on creating a strong workforce and helping individuals develop their minds, their interpersonal skills, and their work ethics through inquiry (Committee on Prospering in the Global Economy of the 21st Century 2006).

What Is Inquiry?

Inquiry is truly different from traditional science teaching practices. In *Inquiry and the National Science Education Standards* (NRC 2000), inquiry is defined by five Essential Features. If students are not engaged in all five features, they are not engaged in inquiry. Column 1 in Table 1.1 lists the five Essential Features, and column 2 describes each feature from *Inquiry and the National Science Education Standards*. The features of traditional teaching are listed in column 3.

Table 1.1

Essential Features of inquiry teaching versus traditional science teaching

	Essential Feature	Description of Essential Features From *Inquiry and the National Science Education Standards*	Traditional Science Teaching
1	Engaging, Scientific Questions	"Learners are engaged by scientifically oriented questions … that lend themselves to empirical investigations, and lead to gathering and using data to develop explanations" (p. 24).	Traditional science teaching typically starts with the facts and ideas of science rather than students' questions and interests.
2	Priority to Evidence	"Learners give priority to evidence, which allows them to develop and evaluate explanations that address scientifically oriented questions" (p. 25).	Data for scientific ideas are absent from most science textbooks and science lectures. Scientific ideas are presented as trustworthy in and of themselves.
3	Explanations From Evidence	"Learners formulate explanations from evidence to address scientifically oriented questions" (p. 26).	Traditional science teachers are the explainers. Students passively receive explanations.
4	Evaluation of Explanations	"Learners … check their results with those proposed by the teacher or instructional materials" (p. 27).	Without features 2 and 3, students have few opportunities to see how scientific ideas best explain natural phenomena.
5	Communicate and Justify Explanations	"Learners communicate and justify their … articulation of the question, procedures, evidence, proposed explanations, and a review of alternative explanations" (p. 27).	Most students find lab reports—the only opportunities that are typically provided for this feature—mystifying and frustrating.

The focus in an inquiry classroom is on what learners are doing, not on what the teacher is doing. Learners are engaged with science topics, putting a priority on evidence and making evaluations of alternative explanations. (See Chapter 2, Table 2.1, p. 18, for additional information on these Essential Features.)

The most important difference between inquiry and traditional science teaching is the third Essential Feature. Learners should be doing the intellectual work of making sense of the data and creating scientific explanations. In traditional instruction, good science teaching is often equated with the teacher presenting a good explanation. In an inquiry classroom, the teacher's role shifts from giving the explanations to supporting students. With the guidance—and even prodding—of their teachers, students must shoulder the intellectual work. Through inquiry, students learn to think.

Inquiry is not merely hands-on teaching. In hands-on science, students may manipulate materials and see scientific evidence, but they are rarely asked to interpret data or engage in the intellectual rigor of creating a scientific explanation. Implementing the Essential Features also requires more than just conducting labs. In traditional instruction, the lab comes after the teacher's explanation of the science concepts and functions as verification. Because they have been told the explanation before the lab even begins, students do not see how scientific explanations develop from evidence nor do they develop the conceptual reasoning skills required when they must analyze scientific explanations.

> **"The focus in an inquiry classroom is on what learners are doing, not on what the teacher is doing."**

The Essential Features also are in stark contrast to the traditional instruction practice of having students listen to a lecture or read the textbook and then answer questions. In such classes, student learning is usually completely divorced from scientific evidence. Traditional lectures and text are not rich with evidence; they focus mainly on the compilation of science ideas, not on the development of those ideas from data. In these classrooms, students have no opportunity to give priority to scientific evidence. Learning science is strictly a matter of having trust in the teacher and the text, rather than seeing science as a set of reasonable, powerful explanations developed from evidence in the natural world.

Inquiry Examples

Let's look at a concrete example of inquiry in the secondary classroom. This example concerns atomic structure and is illustrative of many of the National Science Foundation–supported curriculum materials. (See Chapter 3 for an explanation of how to select curriculum materials supporting the vision of the

National Science Education Standards and Chapter 4 for insights into ways that developers of standards-based curricula carefully consider their tasks when preparing materials to support classroom instruction.)

Think for a moment about the scientific evidence for the existence of atoms and how they are structured. Did you learn this topic in such a way that this evidence quickly comes to mind? Are you struggling to remember any scientific data supporting the ideas of protons, nuclei, electron movement, or other basics of the atomic structure? If you are struggling, imagine how few students could link their knowledge of atomic theory with actual scientific evidence. How many students, instead, take atomic structure more as a matter of faith?

Let's focus on what we know about how electrons move in atoms. This understanding is central to atomic theory, impacting our understanding of atomic size, atomic bonding, and the electromagnetic spectrum. Many science teachers address electron motion through lecture and practice on electron configuration. The traditional instruction sequence looks something like the following:

1. Explain atomic levels 1–7 with some type of visual.
2. Explain sublevels s, p, d, or f with some type of visual.
3. Explain orbitals and their filling order. Give students an order mnemonic, such as $1s^2 \ 2s^2 \ 2p^6 \ 3s^2 \ 3p^6 \ 3d^{10}$ ....
4. Assign practice problems for constructing orbital diagrams of different elements.

Students come away with a basic understanding of electron configuration according to quantum mechanics. Note, though, that throughout the sequence students never encounter evidence for electron configuration or evaluate quantum mechanics as the best explanation for the evidence about the structure of matter.

A second traditional approach adds a verification lab to illustrate the lecture. This instructional sequence can look like the following:

1. Explain electron levels and sublevels.
2. Explain electron movement between energy levels, including energy absorption, emissions, and electron instability.
3. Explain or demonstrate examples of energy emissions.
4. Provide students with a flame-test lab to verify explanations.
    a. Students observe wooden splints soaked in ionic solutions.
    b. Students note color differences when holding splints in a flame.
    c. Students use a flame test to determine the identity of an unknown solution.

The goal of this instructional sequence is to provide a clear explanation of the concepts and then reinforce those concepts with physical examples. If the demonstration or verification lab is conducted, students will see evidence there. Note, though, that the students are placed in an intellectually passive role. The teacher explains the evidence in the lecture and the demonstration. Students' hands are active in the lab, but students are not challenged to make sense of how the data lead to atomic theory because they have already received the explanation.

Active Chemistry (Eisenkraft and Freebury 2003) provides an inquiry-based approach to electron movement. The instructional sequence is the following:

1. The teacher demonstrates the behavior of cathode ray tubes using an old television monitor and a magnet. The students propose an explanation for the evidence and check their explanation against that provided by British physicist J. J. Thomson.
2. Students observe the atomic emission spectrum of hydrogen gas in a spectral tube. Using given wavelength data, students calculate the frequencies of the spectral lines they observed. Students read about Danish physicist Niels Bohr's model of the atom and compare their data with his.
3. Students observe the atomic emission spectrum of a gas other than hydrogen. Students examine a table presenting first and second ionization energies for the first 36 elements and plot the energies in separate colors on the same graph. Students examine the plot for patterns in stability and consider how the data indicate the need for an expansion of the atomic model to include sublevels.

This instructional sequence guides students to see how the modern quantum mechanical explanation of atomic structure arises from and best explains actual data. Note also that students' development of explanations here is scaffolded. Understanding how ionization energies lead to atomic sublevel theory is complex thinking, and students are not put in the role of developing explanations from scratch. Instead, the *Active Chemistry* text consistently guides students to propose explanations for the evidence they have examined in close association with the explanations provided by scientists. During inquiry on many science concepts, especially intellectually rigorous concepts such as quantum mechanics, students are not allowed to wander down dead-end paths.

Inquiry in the Classroom

Inquiry works. I know that—not just because it is supposed to or because the national standards say it does, but because I have seen it at work in my classroom with my students. In the remainder of this chapter, I'll tell you a story to encourage you to add more inquiry to your teaching. My story is a little odd, though, because it starts with my experiences as a science methods teacher at a university.

Sadly, I had become the methods professor that I hoped never to be: I was talking about something I didn't really know anything about. I was telling my preservice teachers how great inquiry was and why they needed to use it. I did not have an answer, however, when they would ask, "So, how does inquiry really work?" I had never used it myself with real students. Until that time, my high school chemistry and physics teaching experience consisted of traditional lectures followed by verification labs. I knew I was in trouble. I realized that I needed to experience inquiry firsthand if I wanted to coach teachers effectively.

During a yearlong sabbatical, I took a job as a regular, full-time teacher in a local public high school teaching ninth-grade physical science. My students were pretty typical: Few liked science, and most were not focused on getting high grades. I did, however, work at a school that supported inquiry teaching. I had supportive teaching colleagues, a supportive administration, and adequate materials. I chose this school so that I could give inquiry a fair test. If inquiry did not work here, I couldn't blame it on the school context.

The year did not start off well. I made a classic mistake that many science teachers make when they first attempt inquiry. I tried to use *open-ended inquiry* right from the start. If you are unfamiliar with that term, you are probably familiar with the idea. It goes something like this:

OK, students, for the next 4–6 weeks we're going to be studying sound and light. On the demonstration table I've placed all of the sound and light equipment the school has. I've also brought in some old musical instruments. I want you to think about something you want to learn about sound and light. Think of a specific question that you're trying to answer. Let me know what you come up with. Then, form yourselves in groups, decide how you're going to experiment, and get busy. Use any of the equipment that you want. Keep good records of what you do and your results. Then, you'll present your findings to me and the rest of the class. OK? Got it? Any questions? Good. Get busy. I'll be floating around to see how I can help you.

As you probably know, this approach does not work. It creates chaos and confusion in most classrooms. I honestly should have known better.

From the first week of school, things steadily got worse. The students began the year somewhat skeptical of the new approach we were trying, but they played along. Four weeks into the semester students began to get frustrated. They did not know how to work in an open-ended inquiry environment, even though many of them were trying. The labs asked them to design procedures but did not give them any support in doing that. They did not have a matching textbook, so at home they weren't sure how to study. They liked the hands-on part of inquiry, but the rest of the learning was a fog.

By October, we were all frustrated. The students felt they were not learning anything, and they were always confused. The teaching team was exhausted from trying to create a standards-based, effective inquiry curriculum from scratch in addition to setting up labs, grading papers, and doing all of our other regular teacher duties.

In November, we attempted yet another open-ended inquiry project, the Free Fall Inquiry. This inquiry was presented to the students as written in Figure 1.1. The goal was for students to see that objects fall at the same rate, regardless of their mass. This inquiry was sheer chaos! Most of the students just played throughout the experience—running up and down the stairs between floors, throwing things at each other from floor-to-floor, and hanging out of the third-floor windows. That lack of safety actually caused the administration to step in and stop the investigation. I was ashamed. One of my students could have gotten hurt in the name of inquiry. The failure of this investigation served as the coup de grâce of open-ended inquiry. I was ready for a new model.

Figure 1.1

Free Fall Inquiry

* Task: Accurately predict the time required for an object to fall from the third floor to the second and first floors.
* Phases of the Inquiry
  * Acceleration overview
  * Initial prediction with group
  * Gathering materials
  * Determining actual distances
  * Finalizing prediction
  * Determining actual time
  * Reflecting and refining the method
  * Reporting

I retreated. I left inquiry (temporarily) and returned to what I knew would work. I did not go back to traditional teaching, though. That had been a failure for me, also, the first time I was teaching high school. Most of my students never really understood chemistry. Sure, most memorized their way to a B or a C grade, but they did not really learn what I was trying to teach. I fell back to a research-based teaching method called Teaching for Conceptual Change (TCC). Using the TCC method, I found out what my ninth graders knew (including their misconceptions), gave them hands-on lab experiences designed to show them key science evidence, and then guided them through a large-group debriefing of the experiment so they could reorganize their ideas based on the evidence they had seen. At the time, I didn't think I was doing inquiry, but now I realize I was.

An example of TCC is the Towel and Spoon lesson. The lesson revolved around the following scenario:

In a kitchen drawer are several items, including a large metal spoon and a dish towel. They have been there overnight. To the touch, the metal spoon feels cold while the towel does not. Why is this so?

The lesson proceeded like this:
1. Present the problem to the students and have them write down their initial ideas.
2. Distribute dish towels and metal kitchen utensils to groups of students. Ask them to explore the equipment and develop initial explanations for what they observe.
3. Show the students a thermometer wrapped in a dish towel and a thermometer bundled between several metal utensils. Note that the temperatures of the two are the same.
4. Through large-group questioning, guide students to see the conflict between the ideas that the metal is cold when its temperature is actually the same as that of the towel.
5. Orchestrate discussion to help students link the following scientific explanations with the evidence from the investigation:
    a. The cold feeling in our fingers results from heat loss due to conduction.
    b. Temperature is average kinetic energy.
    c. With time, all objects in a system come to the same ambient temperature.
    d. There is a difference between heat and temperature.

This lesson worked! The students faced a real conflict in their thinking: How could the metal feel cold when the thermometer showed it to be the same temperature as the towel? This conflict set the stage for serious thinking about the difference between heat and temperature, a concept developed in future lessons in the heat unit. And the students were truly learning. I was surprised again and again by the number of students who were able to explain the science they were seeing in their own words, using their own ideas. Looking back, I see that the basic flow of inquiry was working: With my guidance, students encountered evidence, used it to develop explanations, and evaluated their explanations against the data and one another's ideas to finalize a scientifically sound understanding of the world.

Bolstered by this success, we decided to teach our last unit of the year using a chapter from *Active Physics*. This National Science Foundation–supported curriculum achieved the goals we had been trying unsuccessfully to achieve in the fall. We piloted the "Let Us Entertain You" chapter, focused on sound and light from *Active Physics: Communication*. Things really fell into place. The students were relieved to have a structure to support their learning. They liked having a book.

They liked having labs with instructions. They liked having sections they could read and liked knowing that they were following the same basic structure for each investigation. They finally knew what to expect when they came to class.

They also began to be truly successful with inquiry. By February, they were working effectively in self-directed lab teams. They would come into class, check the whiteboard for lesson modifications, open their books, and start the lab. When they had procedural questions, they asked someone in their group, got an answer, and kept working. I was checking in with the groups, but no one was dependent on me. In fact, I sometimes felt as if I were interrupting their work. I realized then how far my students had come over the year: from passive to active, from waiting to responsible, from disengaged to focused.

They were also learning to think more. I started asking a new question at the beginning of each lab debrief: "What new idea do you think yesterday's lab was designed to show you?" Again and again, my students provided an initial description of the scientific explanation without assistance. They were mastering Essential Feature 3 because they could sort through their prior knowledge, think through the new evidence they had just encountered, and find new ideas they had not encountered before. They were also becoming skillful in proposing and refining ideas in their small groups based on the evidence, as described by Essential Feature 4.

A key success was their use of respectful dialogue. This skill did not come easily, however. Throughout the year, I had to demand that students speak to each other in respectful ways, and I showed zero tolerance for making fun of another person's idea. One way I created this kind of dialogue was by asking groups to post their lab data on 3' × 4' whiteboards with key data on the left side and an explanation of their data on the right. Whiteboards were then placed around the room periphery for easy viewing. I would guide a large-group discussion, in which the students evaluated all of the explanations to determine the one that best fit the data. I insisted that criticisms focus on ideas, not people, as a way to teach respectful dialogue. Students really became skilled at this process. They learned to build on and refine one another's ideas, and they began to see how scientists develop and refine explanations as a community. They also experienced the fine line between constructive criticism of an idea and destructive criticism of a person's character.

My students were also individually learning science content—a key requirement of any approach to science teaching, including inquiry. Evidence of learning existed in both formal assessments and my informal student interactions. Many of the girls who entered the year disconnected from science began to see themselves as able to understand science and saw science as meaningful to their lives. Many of the boys who viewed themselves as academic failures began to discover that they had good common sense about science ideas and good technical skills for science processes. My students with individual education plans were successful in learning science content, a success I attribute to the multimodal learning opportunities provided in an inquiry classroom. As a whole, my students seemed to be retaining the science content in their long-term memories, which I believe was based on their forging a link between abstract science ideas and the memorable concrete experiences of hands-on science.

Returning to Reform

We are in the midst of science education reform because our students need a significantly different preparation for work in a global economy and life in a modern society. Inquiry is at the center of the reforms because traditional instruction is failing American students. Inquiry is not just new jargon or a new fad. Inquiry, as shown by the Essential Features, is actually different from current science teaching.

I hope that my sabbatical story painted a concrete picture of how inquiry can be implemented in a regular classroom. I also hope that you recognize that to introduce inquiry you do not need to totally start over in your teaching. Since my sabbatical year, I have had many opportunities to work with teachers across the country and help them get started with inquiry. Almost always, good science teachers realize that they are already adept at some of the Essential Features. Hands-on teachers already have students encounter evidence, as in Essential Features 1–3. Teachers skilled with creating good classroom dialogue already guide students to hone explanations, as in Essential Features 3 and 4. Teachers skilled with classroom management already have the organization skills essential for managing student work in labs and small-group discussions.

Think of the move toward inquiry as a value-added approach. You already have strengths in your teaching practice. How can inquiry help you add value to what you are already doing? This value is measured in your students achieving new knowledge and skills in their science learning.

Recommended Resources

Bell, R., L. Smetana, and L. Binns. 2005. Simplifying inquiry. *The Science Teacher* 72 (10): 30–33. This article is a quick read that breaks inquiry into four types, many of which will look familiar to science teachers from all backgrounds.

Friedman, T. L. 2005. *The world is flat: A brief history of the twenty-first century.* **New York: Farrar, Straus, and Giroux.** No book gives a better view of the challenges that American students will face in the global economy. Start here if you're still wondering if science teaching really needs to be reformed or if you're not sure what demands your students will face in a global economy.

National Research Council (NRC). 2000. *Inquiry and the National Science Education Standards: A guide for teaching and learning.* This book is the source of the five Essential Features of inquiry. It gives an in-depth look at inquiry, including case studies and assessment ideas. You can read it for free online in either html or PDF form.

2

Reform, One Teacher at a Time

Julie Gess-Newsome, Jackie Mensaco, and
Joëlle Clark
*Center for Science Teaching and Learning,
Northern Arizona University*

An old saying goes, "The only constant is change." No truer words have ever been spoken, especially in a time of reform. As a matter of fact, reform *is* change.

What needs to change in science education? The way teachers think about teaching and learning needs to change (and we include ourselves as teachers). The way we think about the content in our courses and the outcomes we desire for our students need to change too.

The current reforms as outlined in documents such as the *National Science Education Standards* (NRC 1996) and *Project 2061: Science for All Americans* (AAAS 1990) are broad and ambitious, and they impact the entire educational system. The educational system, as is true for all systems, is a synthesis of its parts, however. The most critical component is the classroom teacher. Only when we teachers change will the system change and reform be achieved.

This chapter examines change from two perspectives. The first perspective examines the research on learning because learning involves change. The second perspective examines the change process, highlighting the research and illuminating key ideas surrounding change. At the end of the chapter we will apply the change process to the secondary science classroom context, illustrating the change process, identifying ways to overcome potential barriers, and outlining steps to enact change that will ultimately result in the reform of secondary science education.

Learning and Change

Two books have made a significant impact on our thinking about learning: *How People Learn: Brain, Mind, Experience, and School* (Bransford, Brown, and Cocking 2000) and its companion text, *How Students Learn: Science in the Classroom* (Donovan and Bransford 2005). These books synthesize and link the research on learning to classroom practice. The following four statements link the learning research with reform efforts in science education.

1. Learning with understanding requires organization and application.

Given the same task, experts outperform novices. Why? Although the number of facts known by both individuals may be the same, the expert organizes these facts around a conceptual framework of fundamental ideas. That conceptual framework allows the expert to quickly identify the relevant aspects of a problem and place the problem within an organizational scheme that enhances problem solving. The ability to use knowledge, as opposed to simply restating it, is a feature of learning with understanding.

Science is often taught as a set of isolated facts to be memorized rather than a set of concepts to be applied. Think about the following application example: What do cell division, osmosis, and an elephant's ear have in common? Secondary students may know some facts about cell division and osmosis, maybe even about an elephant's ear. Most would struggle to answer this question, though.

An expert biology teacher would recognize these as specific examples of the relationship between surface area and volume in living systems. A cell divides when the surface area is too small in comparison to its volume to absorb and excrete necessary materials. Rates of osmosis are controlled by surface-area-to-volume ratios, which explains the narrow diameter yet extensive length of the small intestine. And an elephant's ear is one of the animal's primary mechanisms of cooling, with a large, thin, flat surface rich in blood vessels exposed to the air to release heat energy.

A student with a knowledge of surface-area-to-volume relationships now has a conceptual tool that can pull seemingly disparate pieces of information into a connected whole. Once organized, the information can be applied to other contexts, such as recognizing that the effectiveness of an open or closed circulatory system is based on the size of the organism. For true understanding to occur, knowledge must be deep, connected, and organized and be able to be applied in problem-solving situations.

2. Learning is active and social.

To learn for understanding, the learner must collect evidence and make sense of information in order to produce an explanation. Such work is active. Learning cannot be done for someone; learners must do it for themselves. Since learning for understanding involves sense-making, working in a social setting is important. In conversations with others, ideas are transparent and can be examined from multiple points of view. This process assists in both clarifying thinking and verbalizing support for or challenges to the ideas being examined. This characteristic has important implications for teachers and their classrooms. It becomes the responsibility of teachers to create collaborative classroom cultures that encourage and support learners in asking questions, sharing tentative ideas, and solving problems together.

3. Learning requires change.

All students enter our classrooms with ideas about how the world works. These ideas are sometimes in line with scientific explanations and other times are not. Allowing student ideas to go unnoted, however, can have serious consequences for learning. For learning to occur, there must be change. Change can involve adding an idea to preexisting ideas (assimilation) or changing the structure of thinking in order for the idea to fit (accommodation). When preexisting ideas contradict new learning, the new idea can be rejected completely or, more often, remembered just long enough to pass a test!

When students' ideas are made obvious, however, there is an opportunity to refine or replace prior thinking with new ideas. This process is called conceptual change. Conceptual change occurs when a person becomes dissatisfied with his or her current ideas and replaces them with new ideas that better organize and explain the facts.

Conceptual change is hard, both for the student and for the teacher. To teach for understanding, teachers must find ways to uncover student preconceptions and ideas. One obvious way to do this is to ask the student! There are also a number of resources that list commonly held science misconceptions. *Benchmarks for Science Literacy* (AAAS 1993) and *Atlas of Science Literacy* (AAAS 2001) both contain information about common student misconceptions. *Making Sense of Secondary Science* (Driver et al. 1994) similarly lists common misconceptions. These resources will provide valuable knowledge about student thinking and help you understand why, in some cases, learning does not occur.

4. The learning process requires self-monitoring.

An important part of learning is monitoring our own understanding, called metacognition. Metacognition strategies are "self-talk" about the learning process. When we actively question ourselves about what we do and do not understand, what we need to further our learning, and when we have not learned, we can monitor our evolving understanding. For both teachers and students, metacognitive strategies are important skills to learn and practice. We all need to ask ourselves questions such as, "Does this idea make sense? How are these concepts related? Can I restate the idea in my own words? In which situations would this idea apply?"

When students use metacognitive strategies, their misconceptions become apparent to themselves and the teacher. This process opens students' ideas for examination, allows for active monitoring of learning, and results in increased student learning. (See Chapter 1 for additional ideas about implementing conceptual change teaching strategies in the classroom.)

It should be obvious from this review that the vision of reform in secondary science classrooms includes changing our emphasis from what teachers do to what students learn and how their thinking changes as a result of participating in our classrooms. Teachers truly are the key to learning, the key to change, and the key to reform.

The Change Process

If change were simple, we wouldn't need to devote a chapter to it. Change is hard. In their book, *Implementing Change: Patterns, Principles, and Potholes,* Hall and Hord (2001) outline principles of change through the Concerns-Based Adoption Model and offer three tools that can be used to plan and monitor the change process. This section will highlight the key findings about the change process and introduce these three tools.

Change is a process, not an event.

This statement is probably familiar, but what does it mean? When change is viewed as an event, it can be visualized as something that is "done to" someone else. The "change as event" viewpoint is found in the assumption that attending a one-hour inservice after school, or even a one-day inservice at the beginning of the school year, is enough to induce change. We all know this is not true.

The idea is similar to one stated by some teachers: "I taught it; therefore, my students must have learned it." As we know from *How People Learn,* learning is a much more complex process. This is also true for change. By viewing change as a process, we honor the idea that for a big change to occur, many small changes must be stimulated by many other small events recurring over a period of time. To trace the process of change, Hall and Hord recommend using Innovation Configuration (IC) Maps.

An IC Map allows an individual participating in a change to accomplish several things. First, the development of the map provides an opportunity to operationally define what the idealized change would look like when fully implemented. The map consists of a series of brief statements along a continuum describing incremental variations between the existing state and full implementation. This common vision helps all involved recognize how the small steps will eventually result in the desired state. Regular monitoring using an IC Map also helps alert participants to any drift or mutation of the original goals and reminds them of the purposes of the change by describing the major observable components of the change.

When talking about change and reform, people often talk about implementing an innovation. An innovation can be a new teaching style, such as incorporating inquiry into teaching content, adopting a new curriculum, or creating a new culture in which teachers share student work in an effort to improve student learning. An IC Map is a carefully designed description of the innovation and the different steps toward making that innovation part of common practice. Typically, there are 8 to 15 components of an innovation and 2 to 6 variations in each component.

For instance, Table 2.1 (p. 18) is a form of an IC Map describing the potential steps to be taken to introduce more inquiry into a science classroom. (Also see Chapter 1 for concrete examples of inquiry in action.) The cells down the left-hand side describe the five essential features or components of inquiry. For each feature or component, there exists a series of incremental variations, moving from student-directed to teacher-directed inquiry. Each cell paints a picture of what movement toward the successful use of the innovation might look like. For example, one desired outcome is to encourage students to engage in more scientifically oriented questions by generating and posing their own questions.

In a teacher-centered classroom, the teacher poses scientific questions and problems to students. The plan to move toward a student-centered environment includes working with students to select from, refine, and critique teacher-posed questions. An IC Map, therefore, offers a series of benchmarks by which progress in the process of change can be gauged. By designing and evaluating a change innovation using an IC Map, the idea that change is a planned process and not an event is reinforced, and small achievements can be celebrated while keeping an eye on the final goal.

Change involves emotion.

Change means learning new things and adding new knowledge or skills to our repertoire. At these times, change can be exhilarating and extend the boundaries of who we are. Just as in learning and conceptual change, though, not all change means simply adding new insights to current thinking. Sometimes change means letting things go, which can cause frustration, grief, and a sense of disequilibrium and loss.

Let's return to the idea of introducing inquiry-based strategies into science teaching. Although inquiry teaching can be just another strategy added to your teaching tool kit, the philosophy behind inquiry teaching is fundamentally different from the strategies that undergird traditional instruction. For instance,

Table 2.1

Innovation Configuration Map for inquiry-based activities

Essential Features/ Components	Variations			
	(a)	(b)	(c)	(d)
1. Learner engages in scientifically oriented questions	Learner poses a question	Learner selects among questions, poses new questions	Learner sharpens or clarifies question provided by teacher, materials, or other source	Learner engages in question provided by teacher, materials, or other source
2. Learner gives priority to evidence in responding to questions	Learner determines what constitutes evidence and collects it	Learner directed to collect certain data	Learner given data and asked to analyze	Learner given data and told how to analyze
3. Learner formulates explanations from evidence	Learner formulates explanations after summarizing evidence	Learner guided in process of formulating explanations from evidence	Learner given possible ways to use evidence to formulate explanation	Learner provided with evidence and how to use evidence to formulate explanation
4. Learner connects explanations to scientific knowledge	Learner independently examines other resources and forms the links to explanations	Learner directed toward areas and sources of scientific knowledge	Learner given possible connections	
5. Learner communicates and justifies explanations	Learner forms reasonable and logical argument to communicate explanations	Learner coached in development of communication	Learner provided broad guidelines to sharpen communication	Learner given steps and procedures for communication
More	←——— Amount of Learner Self-Direction ———→			Less
Less	←——— Amount of Direction From Teacher or Curriculum Materials ———→			More

Source: National Research Council (NRC). 2000. *Inquiry and the national science education standards: A guide for teaching and learning.* Washington, DC: National Academy Press, p. 29.

past instructional practices were based on the idea of authority, and the teacher or the textbook organized instruction in terms of explanations given to students to learn.

Reform-based teaching shifts from this thinking to a recognition of the power of experience. For students to learn, they need to be involved in the collection of evidence from which they create their own explanations. These reform-based and traditional philosophies are opposed to each other and cannot be held simultaneously. Therefore, to adopt a reform-based approach to teaching and learning, we must let go of previously held—sometimes cherished, comfortable, and efficient—ways of thinking and acting. These changes may not happen all at once, but as IC Maps help us recognize, change requires adjustments both in thinking and behavior.

Shifting toward reform-based science teaching is a significant change accompanied by a natural and developmental process. Hord and Hall describe this developmental pattern of feelings as they evolve during the change process as Stages of Concern. As can be seen in Table 2.2 (p. 20), if we start from the bottom, the Stages of Concern move from concerns for *self*, with a focus on how the intervention will impact the teacher personally, to concerns for the *task*. Task concerns focus on teaching and include the mechanics of implementing the innovation, such as gathering materials, planning, and managing time.

With time and experience, task concerns are replaced with concerns for *impact*, or a focus on student learning. At the impact stage, collaboration with others and an examination of student work results in improved student outcomes and instructional practices. By understanding that we each move through this developmental process as we begin changing our instructional practices, we know that the feelings we experience are normal and shared by others.

Table 2.2 includes language indicating where a teacher's concerns may be when moving to an inquiry-based teaching practice and philosophy. The Stages of Concern model recognizes that individuals do not move cleanly from one stage to another and that concerns will not be limited to one stage. Concerns will, however, cluster in a primary stage at a given time. Recognizing the stages and the emotions corresponding with change can help us know what to expect in the change process, help us identify the type of help required as our needs change, and provide encouragement to persist during times of frustration.

Change requires time and support.

The fact that change takes time may seem obvious, but rarely do we give ourselves enough time to see the change process all the way through. In studies of the change process, researchers have found that even an intervention that is appropriate and has the necessary support may take three to five years to fully implement. That time frame is much different from the one to four years we

Table 2.2

Stages of concern

Concern	Stage of Concern		Teacher Behavior	Characteristic Teacher Comment
Impact	6	Refocusing	Seeks ways that the innovation impacts can be improved	"If we revise our inquiry unit to include more open-ended investigations, I wonder if our students would be more prepared for designing science fair projects?"
	5	Collaboration	Works with others in the implementation of the innovation	"How can we design an inquiry unit on the properties of matter?"
	4	Consequence	Shows interest in how the innovation impacts students	"Wow! My students really seem to be more engaged when I use inquiry lessons!"
Task	3	Management	Considers how to implement the innovation in terms of organization, time management, and efficiency	"I'm not sure where I'm going to find the time to collect the materials to do inquiry-based teaching."
Self	2	Personal	Considers what involvement with the innovation will mean on a personal level	"I wonder if inquiry-based teaching strategies would work for me."
	1	Informational	Shows willingness to learn more, but has no direct involvement	"What is inquiry? What does it look like in the science classroom?"
	0	Awareness	Demonstrates little information, concern, or involvement	"What's the big deal about inquiry?"

Source: Adapted from Hall, G.E., and S. M. Hord. 2001. *Implementing change: Patterns, principles and potholes.* Needham Heights: MA: Allyn and Bacon, p. 63.

generally give ourselves to make a change. And the change process can be unduly complicated if we are trying to implement multiple changes at the same time.

Actions related to the change process follow a predictable pattern with similarities to the Stages of Concern. Hall and Hord (2001) developed Levels of Use to recognize differences between users and nonusers of an innovation (see Table 2.3, p. 22). Let's continue with the example of introducing inquiry-based strategies into science teaching. Nonusers have limited interaction with the innovation, but they may be spending important time learning about specific strategies that encourage learners to pose their own testable questions and considering how to begin to use those strategies in the classroom. Users have moved beyond preparation and have made the decision to take on the challenge of trying out these inquiry-based strategies. Users in their early attempts at putting the new strategies into practice may feel awkward and sense that they are spending a great deal of time constantly referring to their lesson plans or notes for guidance and reassurance.

Often, the innovation can fail at this mechanical level of use. Frustrations can arise unless there is support. As teachers try new strategies, coaching or teacher-partners can help overcome these frustrations. As in any kind of learning, changes in practice are best supported in a social environment. Such support can be helpful, especially when the new practice falls into the "implementation dip," where comfort levels are low, and student learning outcomes may actually get worse. With time and practice, however, the new strategies become familiar and used on a routine basis. Student learning results will improve, and with student learning data in hand, additional refinements to the intervention can be made.

Steps Toward Change

So, are you ready to take steps toward reforming your classroom practice? Consider the following steps:

Visualize the change.

The first step toward reform is knowing what you want to change. Think about teaching and learning in your classroom. What issues concern you? Are you happy with the level of inquiry in your science instruction? If not, increasing inquiry-based activities from once a month to once a week may be a place to start.

How are your English language learners faring compared with your native speakers? Maybe you could adopt three new strategies that have been shown to meet the needs of this population. Or maybe you could pilot a unit from a new set of curriculum materials or identify and address student misconceptions in an upcoming unit. Pick something you care about and start small.

Table 2.3

Levels of use of an innovation

Use	Levels of Use		Teacher Behavior
Users	VI	Renewal	Re-evaluates materials and may revise or replace them in order to increase impact
	V	Integration	Seeks collective impact by working with others
	IVB	Refinement	Makes minor changes to increase the impact of the innovation on student learning
	IVA	Routine	Shows ease of use of the innovation as designed
	III	Mechanical Use	Focuses on day-to-day use of the innovation with limited time for reflection
Nonusers	II	Preparation	Prepares to use the innovation
	I	Orientation	Begins stages of learning about the innovation
	0	Nonuse	Has little or no knowledge of the innovation

Source: Adapted from Hall, G.E., and S. M. Hord. 2001. *Implementing change: Patterns, principles and potholes.* Needham Heights: MA: Allyn and Bacon, p. 82.

Once you've determined what you want to do, consider crafting an Innovation Configuration Map to guide your work and trace your success. For instance, if you want to increase the number of inquiry-based activities in your classroom, construct a map that traces your progress toward your ideal, such as the one in Table 2.4. Of course, you would need to complete the rest of the IC Map, describing the elements of inquiry important to you, and you would need to define what inquiry in the classroom looks like, as was done in Table 2.1.

Table 2.4

Innovation Configuration Map for inquiry activities

Component 1: Degree of use of inquiry instruction				
(a)	(b)	(c)	(d)	(e)
Inquiry activities used more than once each week	Four inquiry activities used each month	Three inquiry activities used each month	Two inquiry activities used each month	One inquiry activity used each month

Find support.

Learning is social and active, and change is best attempted in a supportive environment. Identify individuals and opportunities that can help assist you in supporting your change plans. Perhaps a colleague has similar concerns about making instructional changes, and you can coach each other through the process. Professional development providers, such as a faculty member in a local university or a science coordinator in your district, could offer guidance and support. Or, in the case of well-designed curriculum materials, the materials themselves may act as a source of support.

Be patient.

Remember, change takes time and practice. In the process, you may experience emotions of elation and frustration, joy and grief. Recognize that these feelings are to be expected and are part of the process of moving from concerns about self, to those of task, and then to impact on student learning. It takes time to learn to do something new, but with practice, awkward and self-conscious moves become fluid and natural. Trace your own movement through the Stages of Concern and Levels of Use as you move from personal and management concerns in the use of your chosen innovation to more collaborative and refined forms of implementation.

Collect evidence.

Inquiry is about collecting evidence and seeking explanation. Many of the recommendations of reform, including those in this book, may feel like the explanations created by others. But learning is something *we* do, not what others do to us. Design opportunities to collect your own data to determine if the explanations for reform are borne out in your school setting. What would success look like? Improved student learning on a test? Higher levels of student motivation as demonstrated by attendance? Increased understanding as demonstrated by improved class discussions? Determine the data that will help convince you of the student benefits realized by changing your practice, and examine that data. Remember, though, change takes time and learning gains will not be immediate.

Examine the process.

Track your personal progress in making change by examining your IC Map. Continually ask yourself what concerns you have about the change you are making in order to help you understand your emotional reactions to the process. Pay constant attention to the teaching behaviors you are exhibiting to determine your level of reformed classroom practice. By reflecting on and noting your progress, you will have opportunities to celebrate successes and analyze your challenges. Use these challenges to determine how you may be able to do things differently or identify missing sources of support. In the process, you will be learning more about the change process and improving your classroom practice in order to improve student learning. You will be actualizing the goal of reform and will be contributing to its success.

Change happens, one teacher at a time!

Recommended Resources

Bransford, J. D., A. L. Brown, and R. R. Cocking. 2000. *How people learn: Brain, mind, experience, and school.* Washington, DC: National Academy Press. A synthesis of the research on learning and teaching with special attention on ways the research findings can and should impact classroom practice. A must-read for all teachers.

Donovan, M. S., and J. D. Bransford, eds. 2005. *How students learn: Science in the classroom.* Washington, DC: National Academies Press. Specific science examples that highlight the findings from *How People Learn.*

Driver, R., A. Squires, P. Rushworth, and V. Wood-Robinson. 1994. *Making sense of secondary science: Research into children's ideas.* New York: Routledge Press. A compendium of student misconceptions organized by topic area.

Hall, G. E., and S. M. Hord. 2001. *Implementing change: Patterns, principles, and potholes.* Needham Heights, MA: Allyn and Bacon. A highly readable explanation of the principles of change and an in-depth presentation of the Concerns-Based Adoption Model. Also discusses facilitation of and leadership in reform.

THE ROLE OF CURRICULUM IN SCIENCE EDUCATION REFORM

3

The Role of Curriculum Materials in Reform

Joseph A. Taylor, April L. Gardner, and Rodger W. Bybee
Biological Sciences Curriculum Study (BSCS)

D o curriculum materials have a role in science education reform? The following vignette illustrates how curriculum materials are traditionally selected and used.

Vignette 1: Physics in District USA

When Mr. Chen arrived as the physics teacher at West Lake High School, he used the available textbook to develop and sequence lectures on selected physics topics. Where his content knowledge was strong, Mr. Chen had few problems finding investigations from other sources that would reliably help students verify the science principles he covered in his lectures. Where his background knowledge was weak, Mr. Chen elected to skip those topics. Mr. Chen's usual preference was to cover the key concepts in his lectures, spend a few days verifying them with investigations, assign a weekly set of homework problems, and then conclude with a test. After five years, Mr. Chen had a refined set of lectures based on his favorite topics in physics, sets of relevant homework problems, and a large number of investigations.

In Mr. Chen's sixth year, his department head asked him if he wanted to purchase new curriculum materials. Mr. Chen quickly responded that he had worked hard on his physics program and was just now getting it where he wanted it. "Physics is physics. I don't need to use another textbook's definition of kinetic energy," he said. Therefore, if new curriculum materials were mandatory, he preferred to simply purchase the latest edition of the current textbook.

Mr. Chen's story is all too common. Curriculum materials, even those that can organize daily instruction, are pulled off the shelf and used infrequently and haphazardly as a mere resource or supplement. Even skilled and experienced teachers see curriculum materials as helpful but not integral to the learning experiences of students. The frequent result is a patchwork approach to curriculum implementation, which leads to lack of coherence in the learning sequence for students (Rutherford 2000; Taylor et al. 2005). As in the case of Mr. Chen, the notion of teacher as curriculum developer or curriculum "hunter and gatherer" is prevalent.

Several external factors discourage faithful use of curriculum materials, including their lack of alignment with standards and high-stakes state assessments. Teachers are more likely to use curriculum materials with fidelity when the materials align with standards and help prepare students for state assessments. In the absence of a single program meeting all of these needs, many teachers resort to hunting and gathering activities from a variety of sources that collectively appear to address standards and state assessment.

Why Does Curriculum Matter?

Why all the fuss about curriculum materials? What is wrong with searching among a variety of sources for materials that match your strengths and appear to align with the district's standards? Does it really matter which curriculum materials you use?

The short answer is *curriculum materials make a difference.* They influence *what* content is taught and *how* it is taught, which, in turn, affects students' science achievement.

The evidence for the preceding assertions comes from international tests of science concepts. We are no longer surprised to hear that U.S. students rank among the bottom half of the nations participating in these tests. This is true even when comparisons are made between similar students in participating countries. Why do these results exist? One explanation comes from a comparison of curriculum materials and practices in the United States with those of top-ranked countries (Schmidt et al. 2001). U.S. instructional materials include far more topics, introduce those topics earlier in schooling, and cover them much more superficially than instructional materials from the top-ranked countries. Obviously, curriculum materials impact student achievement. Thus, careful selection and faithful implementation of carefully developed curriculum materials have a great potential for promoting science education reform.

Curriculum materials also influence science teachers' understanding of concepts. In fact, the scope of topics addressed in district-mandated materials was found to be the most powerful factor in determining areas of strength in the knowledge base of high school teachers—and presumably the content they taught to their students (Arzi and White 2004).

In the 1990s, a number of scientists and science teachers worked together on two different projects to determine which concepts all students should understand by the time they finished high school. The recommendations reported in *Benchmarks for Science Literacy* (AAAS 1993) and in *National Science Education Standards* (NRC 1996) are remarkably consistent. Together they provide powerful guidance for identifying the most significant science concepts. Curriculum materials based on these standards will encourage teachers to understand and teach the most important science concepts.

Many science curriculum materials cover an exhaustive list of science topics. Standards-based curriculum materials, however, focus in greater depth on the smaller number of concepts recommended by the standards documents. More rigorous development of a smaller number of fundamental concepts more effectively develops the conceptual understanding that leads to greater science achievement. The following vignette illustrates the impact that standards-based instructional materials can have on both student and teacher learning.

Vignette 2: Biology in District USA

When Ms. Johnson arrived at East Valley High School, the school had just adopted a new standards-based biology program. She was expected to use the program's materials to organize her entire year's instruction and to use the specified pedagogical approaches based on research about how people learn. The student textbook had many activities and investigations but fewer reading selections than anything Ms. Johnson had used before. Just as she began to match her previously developed lectures and activities to the new program, she attended a district-sponsored workshop designed to support teachers in their use of the new program. There she experienced several of the activities and investigations as a learner and began to develop an understanding of the rationale and learning goals for the program. Additional workshops supported her as she learned a new way to use curriculum materials, including assistance in areas where her background was the weakest. Ms. Johnson resolved to teach the curriculum as presented and found that over the years her skill in using the pedagogical strategies associated with the program increased. For example, it became routine for her to organize students into cooperative learning teams, provide opportunities for her to identify students' prior understandings about a topic, and conduct ongoing, informal assessment activities that guided further instruction within a chapter.

Ms. Johnson initially felt awkward using the questions and problems in the instructional materials but she used them anyway. Asking students to restate what they had learned and what they still did not understand seemed pointless, but she was surprised and gratified to discover that such questions engaged students more in the learning process. Student questions were more specific and their attitudes were more positive and enthusiastic than those of her previous students. The investigations in the textbook supported the concepts developed in each chapter well—saving her many hours of searching for and developing labs. Following the curriculum materials, she introduced each chapter with a short activity, discussion, or reading, and then launched students into a more in-depth investigation. Using evidence from the investigations, information from the textbooks, and short lectures, students developed explanations for biological phenomena. Ms. Johnson then guided her students in further investigations that extended their understanding. After using the new program for three years, Ms. Johnson was amazed to discover not only how much more biology her students were learning, but also how much she herself had learned about teaching and biology. Furthermore, she found that she now enjoyed teaching more than ever before.

In Chapter 1, Lee Meadows described the frustration he experienced as he tried to design, develop, and teach inquiry-based science activities. He also related how using *Active Physics*, a standards-based program, freed him to focus more on student learning than on curriculum development. Ms. Johnson had a similar experience. Her story further illustrates how the design of standards-based curriculum materials influences what and how we teach and, thus, holds great promise for improving student achievement in science.

What Do Standards-Based Curriculum Materials Look Like?

How can you identify standards-based curriculum materials? Many publishers will argue that their science programs are standards-based because their textbook covers all of the concepts (and then some) mentioned in the National Science Education Standards. "Standards-based" means far more than chapter titles that repeat the labels for the content standards. A truly standards-based program has the following features:

* Includes in-depth instruction on the "big ideas" from the National Science Education Standards
* Sequences those ideas in ways that promote coherent understanding of science concepts
* Uses an inquiry orientation for teaching that develops students' understanding of scientific inquiry, as well as their abilities in scientific inquiry
* Uses student-student and student-teacher discussions for discussing the evidence from investigations and developing explanations of scientific phenomena
* Incorporates informal, ongoing assessments to guide further instruction
* Provides opportunities for students to reflect on what they learned and how they learned it

Research on how people learn was discussed in Chapter 2, and those findings characterize reform-based curriculum materials. Three key findings are paraphrased in the left column of Table 3.1. The right column lists the implications of each finding for curriculum materials (Powell, Short, and Landes 2002).

Distinguishing between standards-based curriculum materials and others requires considerable expertise in science content and pedagogy. Research suggests that even experienced teachers may not recognize how standards-based

Table 3.1

Implications of *How People Learn** for the design of curriculum materials

We know that student learning . . .	So curriculum materials should . . .
is affected by the current concepts that students have about phenomena.	* have a sequence that reveals students' current concepts. * provide opportunities and time for students to replace inaccurate and/or incomplete concepts with more accurate and complete concepts.
requires both facts and a framework in which to place those facts.	* be based on fundamental science concepts. * connect facts to these concepts.
is enhanced by self-reflection and monitoring of learning.	* be explicit about learning objectives and outcomes. * incorporate opportunities for students to develop skill in thinking about how they learned in their lessons.

*Bransford, J. D., A. L. Brown, and R. R. Cocking, eds. 2000. *How people learn: Brain, mind, experience and school.* Washington, DC: National Academy Press.

instruction can be embodied in materials (NRC 1999). Thus, distinguishing standards-based curriculum materials from others requires a systematic process that includes analysis techniques revealing key differences. In the following section, such a process—AIM (Analyzing Instructional Methods)—is outlined. (See the BSCS website at *http://bscs.org/AIM* to learn more about the details of curriculum materials selection.)

Analyzing Instructional Materials (AIM)

AIM is both a process and a collection of tools for analyzing curriculum materials based on criteria from the National Science Education Standards. The process can lead to the selection of curriculum materials or be used as a vehicle for curriculum-based professional development. The current version of the AIM process and tools was developed by BSCS based on the original work of the K–12 Alliance, a division of WestEd.

The AIM process has five basic steps:

1. Identify criteria based on a district's goals, standards, and curriculum framework
2. Prescreen materials
3. Complete a "paper screen" (i.e., a thorough review of materials)
4. Test the materials in the classroom
5. Select curriculum materials (if one's school is using AIM for curriculum selection)

If the process is used for curriculum selection, we recommend taking at least one full academic year to complete the process. A year allows sufficient time for conducting appropriate preselection of professional development, a prescreen of 5 to 10 programs, a full paper screen of the remaining candidates, and a classroom test of up to two programs.

1. Identify criteria.

Many reviewers of curriculum materials think only about the content required by their district or state standards. Although content alignment is important, it is not the only criterion to consider. What about conceptual connections? What about involving students in scientific investigations? How are students assessed? Do the materials help teachers address student preconceptions? AIM challenges those involved in the analysis to develop common understandings about the curriculum materials that go far beyond content alignment with standards.

Because curriculum materials play such an important role in student learning, teachers must work together to identify specific criteria for those materials *before* opening the first book. Questions guiding this step of the AIM process include

* What aspects of curriculum materials enhance the learning process for students?
* What are the characteristics of curriculum materials that best support teachers?

2. Prescreen materials.

After developing a list of criteria for curriculum materials, the curriculum selection/analysis team must select the two or three criteria most important to them. These central criteria frame the *prescreen* process. Next, the team should prescreen all available materials by carefully checking both student and teacher materials for evidence of these must-have criteria. For example, the team may decide that evidence of inquiry-based experiences is essential, along with the following additional criteria: adequate support for teachers in terms of content background, examples of common student misconceptions, materials and supplies, and the use of an instructional model. If a program does not incorporate these must-have criteria, then it should not be considered for further review. Because AIM is in-depth, evidence based, and iterative, the prescreening process is essential to narrowing the field to the three or four sets of curriculum materials most likely to succeed in meeting the district's criteria. This way, the team can spend its time and energy on a thorough look at the remaining materials through the paper screen and classroom testing.

3. Complete a "paper screen."

Following the prescreen, the team should conduct a thorough review (or "paper screen") of the remaining materials. During this procedure, four rubrics should be applied to selected units. The paper screen is most useful when comparing similar units across programs (e.g., comparing the plate tectonics unit from Program 1 with the plate tectonics unit from Program 2).

The rubrics in the AIM process are titled Science Content, Work Students Do, Assessment, and Work Teachers Do. These four categories include most criteria identified by the majority of other districts and are designed to help distinguish standards-based materials from others. The rubrics are used to generate a numeric "score" for each set of curriculum materials so that programs can be compared.

As a first step in making evidence visible, the team should construct a graphic organizer illustrating the flow of the concepts in the selected unit of instruction. A conceptual flow graphic is built by identifying the science concepts in the unit and displaying the strength of connections between the concepts. The result is a large chart filled with the big ideas of the unit (usually written on sticky notes) connected by arrows of varying sizes demonstrating strong or weak relationships (see Figure 3.1, p. 34). The most challenging—and most powerful— part of this process is basing the concepts and linkages in the conceptual flow graphic on evidence from the curriculum materials themselves, rather than on how individual teachers might teach the lessons. This process challenges teachers to think about the content from a learner's perspective and often results in a deepening of a teacher's science content understanding.

Next, the team applies the rubrics to the conceptual flow graphic, looking for evidence of science content, work students do, assessment, and work teachers do. Using evidence from the curriculum materials, the team should justify each score and provide comments about the strengths and limitations for each rubric row. The Science Content rubric includes evidence of standards alignment and scientific accuracy, conceptual development, and appropriate connections among the concepts students are to learn. The Work Students Do rubric assesses the quality of the learning experiences, such as whether students have opportunities to develop the abilities of scientific inquiry and whether the curriculum materials

Figure 3.1

Sample conceptual flow graphic

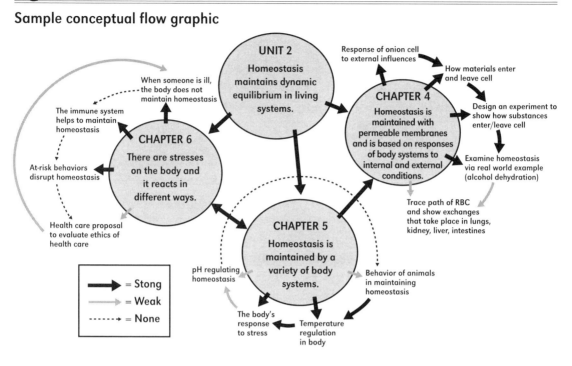

are accessible to all students. This process of carefully examining materials and documenting evidence continues as the team applies the other two rubrics. If a program scores poorly on two rubrics, there is usually no point in continuing with additional rubrics.

4. Test the materials in the classroom.

After the choices have been narrowed down (usually to two sets of curriculum materials), the materials undergo the final test—a classroom pilot test. During this pilot test, teachers should collect data on student learning and ease of implementation by examining student work and using the four rubrics listed in "Complete a 'Paper Screen'." To make a truly evidence-based decision, materials must be tried out in various classrooms. By piloting at least one unit from each program, the pilot team can concretely discuss, contrast, and score the piloted materials based on student learning of important concepts and on teacher instructional support. These data are then applied to additional rubrics that determine a pilot score for each set of materials. The data from the paper screen and the pilot test combine to provide an evidence-based comparison of curriculum materials for use in curriculum selection.

Preparing for AIM

If you are considering purchasing new materials, we suggest that you immediately take certain steps. Professional development is one key step. The Curriculum Topic Study process is a useful starting point for examining how the National Science Education Standards are embodied in curriculum materials (Keeley 2005). Professional development that addresses research on learning and challenges beliefs about the role of curriculum materials is useful in developing common understandings among colleagues. Preselection of professional development can include sessions that build awareness of available standards-based curriculum materials, as well as sessions whose facilitation uses standards-based teaching strategies (e.g., inquiry-based strategies).

Another critical step is involving teachers in examining student work, achievement, and enrollment data to evaluate the impact of the current science program. This enlightening experience can challenge beliefs, help build a shared vision of learning and teaching, and reinforce the need for curricular change.

All members of the curriculum selection team should be included in the professional development. Ideally, this team would include individuals who have a variety of perspectives. For example, the team should include representatives from all schools affected by the selection, including both new and experienced teachers. Each person brings unique and important perspectives on how curriculum materials can support teaching. Don't forget special education staff and reading specialists. They can help the team consider whether the curriculum materials are accessible to all learners.

The AIM process, taken as a whole, has many of the elements scholars suggest are necessary to anchor a *transformative* professional development program—that is, a program that transforms the knowledge, beliefs, and practices of teachers (Thompson and Zeuli 1999). As a result of using AIM to analyze curriculum materials, teachers gain insights into the continuity and depth of standards-based curriculum materials and a better understanding of learning and teaching science. Throughout the process, teachers work collaboratively to discuss their thinking, collect and examine evidence, and apply new beliefs and understandings to classroom practice. In this way, the AIM process becomes a transformative professional development experience because teachers will likely change their knowledge and beliefs about the nature of science, teaching, and learning. Research shows that deep learning can result when a selection process encourages an in-depth analysis of materials that requires applying knowledge of the standards (Brearton and Shuttleworth 1999).

The following vignette illustrates the use of the AIM process to bring about transformative professional development.

Vignette 3: Chemistry in District USA

Mr. Olivas, a chemistry teacher at North Cliff High School, was not surprised at his appointment to the curriculum selection committee. As a 20-year teaching veteran, he had been through the curriculum adoption cycle many times before. At the first committee meeting, he was surprised to see not only three of his chemistry colleagues, but also the district science coordinator and eight chemistry teachers from the other two high schools in the district. The science coordinator addressed the group: "As you know, we have another year before we adopt a new chemistry textbook. But I've learned about a more structured curriculum selection process. Instead of a duty or chore, this curriculum selection can be a professional development opportunity for all of us." Mr. Olivas was doubtful, but he wanted to know more.

The science coordinator went on to explain that the committee would use a rigorous process leading to an evidence-based decision about the chemistry program that would best support their student learning goals. The process included piloting units from prospective programs and a three-week summer contract for teachers who wanted to participate. Intrigued, three teams of teachers formed from the participating schools.

The teachers were surprised to learn that they would not be looking at textbooks right away. Instead, they held several meetings to reach consensus on the critical criteria for a new program. The agreement needed to attend to district goals, not just individual preferences. Mr. Olivas realized that he had never thought about curriculum adoption in this way before and was energized by the discussions. As one colleague said, "This is really what teaching is about—identifying the most significant chemistry concepts and working with colleagues to come up with the best ways to help our students learn those concepts." The others agreed; seldom had such important discussions taken place. By the end of the school year, the teams had agreed on two major required criteria and had refined a set of rubrics that would help them collect evidence on how well a program supported their teaching and learning objectives.

During the summer, an initial screening of nine prospective chemistry programs was quickly completed using the two major criteria identified. Three programs survived. Each of those programs was examined in depth, and evidence was collected for the rubrics. This process was occasionally contentious. Sometimes the teachers had to stop to review what would count as evidence; other times they found themselves in deep discussions about the significance of a particular activity or the sequence of activities for learning a specific chemistry concept. Once the rubrics were completed, they scored each program for the match between its features and their district teaching and learning objectives.

Midway through the summer work, Mr. Olivas commented, "This really is professional development! I can't remember the last time I had such rich discussions about chemistry—and especially about teaching chemistry. I've got some great ideas from my colleagues, and I think I gave them some insights too. This process is about much more than selecting a textbook!"

By the end of the summer the teams had narrowed the field of possible chemistry programs to two. Each teacher would pilot two units from each program during the following school year, which would include collecting more evidence based on actual classroom experience and student work. Mr. Olivas was enthusiastic about pilot testing and was confident that his students would benefit from using these materials. Nevertheless, during the pilot test he was astonished at how involved his students were. He had seldom seen students so excited about chemistry. Furthermore, they seemed to understand chemistry at a conceptual level, instead of merely memorizing definitions and algorithms for solving problems. Mr. Olivas and his colleagues felt confident that next spring they would be able to make an evidence-based decision about the best possible chemistry program for their school.

Conclusions

Although standards-based curriculum materials look very different from other materials, they can act as an overarching organizer of instruction and truly make a difference in student learning when used as designed and supported with professional development. Through analyzing materials, teachers become more skilled at identifying and thinking critically about the effectiveness of standards-based curriculum materials. More important, curriculum materials can influence both the content and the way teachers teach. Standards-based materials focus on the most significant science concepts, as identified by scientists and science educators in the Benchmarks and the National Science Education Standards. These materials also incorporate teaching strategies consistent with current research-based understandings about how people learn. Thus, faithful use of standards-based curriculum materials can be a powerful mechanism for science education reform.

Recommended Resources

Keeley, P. 2005. *Science curriculum topic study.* **Thousand Oaks, CA: Corwin Press.** Curriculum Topic Study (CTS) describes a systematic process and set of tools for examining nearly 150 science topics. This book draws on influential science education resources, such as the Benchmarks and the National Science Education Standards. Teachers can use CTS to identify the big ideas in science, draw connections among major concepts, and increase opportunities for all students to learn science.

Powell, J., J. Short, and N. Landes. 2002. Curriculum reform, professional development, and powerful learning. In *Learning science and the science of learning*, ed. R. Bybee, 121–136. Arlington, VA: NSTA Press. This chapter describes how curriculum selection and analysis can be used as the context for transformative professional development.

Thompson, C. L., and J. S. Zeuli. 1999. The frame and the tapestry. In *Teaching as the learning profession: Handbook of policy and practice*, eds. L. Darling-Hammond and G. Sykes, 341–375. San Francisco: Jossey-Bass. This chapter describes the necessary characteristics for professional development to support the transformation of teacher knowledge, beliefs, and practices into those that are consistent with national standards.

Learning From Innovative Instructional Materials and Making Them Your Own

Jacqueline S. Miller and Ruth Krumhansl
Center for Science Education,
Education Development Center, Inc. (EDC)

Consider the following fictionalized scenario based on discussions with a teacher piloting the use of two curricula developed by the Education Development Center, Inc.—*Insights in Biology* and *Foundation Science.*

Theresa Michaelson has taught chemistry for 15 years in a large suburban high school in the Midwest where chemistry is required for every 10th grader. She majored in chemistry in college and loves her subject. She teaches several levels of chemistry, including AP. She uses different textbooks in every class and works diligently to gear the curriculum toward the needs, abilities, and interests of the students in each class. Every year, to her delight, a few of her students recognize the beauty of chemistry and are inspired by her enthusiasm to pursue it further. And every year she is baffled by the majority of students who find chemistry boring, too hard, and irrelevant.

Last year, her district adopted a new chemistry curriculum for 10th grade. Described as innovative, the curriculum is based on the latest understandings about how students learn. Content is developed as a set of related, cumulative concepts rather than as a set of discrete facts and ideas. It is presented in a real-world context, assessments require students to apply their understandings, and the instructional materials are accompanied by extensive teacher guides. The district's goal was to have more students achieve the learning outcomes prescribed by the state frameworks. District leaders also felt that these innovative instructional materials would engage more students in studying chemistry and in taking more science courses. Adoption of this new curriculum was seen as a major step in reforming science instruction.

The curriculum came with strings attached, however. Because these materials were developed by experts in chemistry and embodied research on effective teaching and learning strategies, district leaders requested that the teachers teach the materials exactly as presented, with no modifications or supplementation.

Theresa had many questions and concerns: How can one curriculum fit all students? What about the expertise in content and pedagogy I bring to my teaching? How can one curriculum respond to the diverse needs of students in my classes or the variability in different classrooms? She reluctantly agreed to teach the materials as written for one year; at the end of the school year she would assess the impact of the curriculum on her students and on herself to decide her course for the following year.

Theresa had many other questions: Who wrote the curriculum? How did they make their choices about content and instructional strategies? Who is their intended audience? How do they intend their materials to be used? What is the impact of these materials on student learning? What role do these curricular materials play in enhancing student learning and interest in science and in helping me develop new approaches to teaching chemistry? How can my own expertise in both subject matter and in teaching work with these materials?

This chapter will explore Theresa's questions, focusing particularly on her last two:

* Can these materials help teachers develop new approaches to teaching and learning? If so, how?
* What role does a teacher's experience, knowledge, and skills, both in content and in teaching, play in implementing these innovative instructional materials?

This chapter will also examine the balance between implementing the materials as written by the developers, on the one hand, and adapting and modifying them in response to teacher and student needs and district requirements, on the other.

Most science educators strongly believe that innovative instructional materials can transform the way science is taught. Such materials can help teachers gain new understandings about how students learn science, including by learning new ways to vary instructional and assessment strategies and by developing new approaches to content and development of conceptual understandings. As this chapter will discuss, however, change is dependent on how the materials are designed. First, the materials must clearly communicate the *intended* curriculum. Second, they must accommodate *teachers' desires to apply their own expertise and style* to a prepared curriculum. Third, they must be written so that, as teachers modify the materials into their *enacted* curriculum, the core philosophy and pedagogy of the materials can be preserved.

Innovative Instructional Materials

Over the past two decades, the National Science Foundation (NSF) has supported the development of a variety of innovative instructional materials featuring new approaches to teaching and learning based on current understandings about how students learn science (see Chapter 2 for details). At the secondary level, NSF has supported the development of several high school science programs, including *Chemistry in the Community*; *Active Physics*; *Biology: A Community Context*; *Physics That Works*; *Insights in Biology*; *EarthComm*; and *BSCS Biology: A Human Approach*. (See the Recommended Resources on p. 49 for a list of guides to innovative curriculum.) The materials are most often developed by teams that include curriculum writers, scientists, teachers, and educational researchers.

These curricula share several common characteristics:

* Content that is scientifically accurate and up-to-date and that provides in-depth explorations of major topics and concepts
* Contexts relevant to students' lives
* Hands-on and inquiry-based instructional strategies that acknowledge varied learning styles
* Emphasis on problem-solving skills and the use of evidence in reaching conclusions
* Assessment strategies embedded in the learning experience, related to the context, informative to the learning as it proceeds, and linked to the learning objectives

These materials are designed to provide students with rigorous and in-depth learning experiences and to facilitate student learning in a progressive path from baseline knowledge to a higher level of conceptual understanding. More recently, these curricula are also being designed to support teachers in incorporating new teaching practices into their instruction.

Ideally, developers of innovative instructional materials strive to meet the expectations and needs of teachers like Theresa. As they create their instructional materials, developers align the materials with national standards and state frameworks, identifying learning outcomes for students (i.e., what content students should know and what they should be able to do to demonstrate achievement of these outcomes). They create a meaningful conceptual flow to connect the content and to scaffold understanding of fundamental principles (see Chapter 3, p. 34) for an example of a conceptual flow graphic). They ensure scientific accuracy.

The materials provide learning experiences that frame student learning in a context that is meaningful to them and that enables all students to achieve the desired learning outcomes. Suggested instructional strategies are varied to address the diverse learning styles and needs of a wide range of students. The strategies give students ample opportunities to explore their ideas through reading, writing, and discussion and to develop skills in explaining their conclusions using evidence and logical thought processes. The materials take into consideration students' prior knowledge and preconceptions. Ideally, teacher guides clearly communicate to teachers the rationales, goals, and strategies inherent in the materials and enable teachers to implement the materials with fidelity to the philosophy, pedagogy, and spirit intended by the developers. At the same time, developers must acknowledge teachers' expertise, beliefs, and needs. Finally, the materials should both increase teachers' knowledge in specific instances of instructional decision making and help teachers develop more general knowledge they can apply flexibly in new situations (Davis and Krajcik 2005). That is, the materials should support teachers in developing new approaches to teaching and in adapting the materials to meet their needs.

Innovative Curricula as an Instrument of Change

Teachers have great influence on how students learn science in the secondary classroom. Although most states have identified learning goals in their state frameworks, many teachers retain significant control over the method of achieving these objectives in their classrooms—the sequencing of content, the pacing of their courses, and the assessment and instructional strategies used to present the materials. Teachers most often turn to textbooks to help them frame and design their courses. The textbook provides a structure, a pathway through the content, and a resource for student readings and activities. Some teachers use textbooks as an exact road map through the material; others use them solely to augment instructional materials they design.

Because teachers rely on textbooks, innovators believe that changes in curricula will spark changes in instruction. The strategy of using innovative curricula to effect change in high school science education, however, has not always been successful. After all, each teacher has a highly individual interpretation of the materials and makes his or her own choices about elements to use or change. Brown and Edelson (2003) examined the ways that teachers interact with curricular materials, specifically the interaction between teacher practice and curricular innovations. Their basic premise was that "regardless of intent [of the developers], teachers invariably notice and use different elements of curricular designs as they customize them to their idiosyncratic needs and contexts" (p. 1). Their study showed that teachers' interpretations of the design and features of innovative materials are greatly influenced by their own backgrounds, knowledge, and skills. The experience of the Educational Development Center's (EDC) Center for Science Education (CSE) over the past four years with teachers from more than 500 U.S. school districts confirms this observation. Although the same innovative materials may be present in classrooms, teachers modify and adapt them in a variety of ways to meet the needs of their students and their own beliefs about good teaching.

The issue of implementation fidelity versus adaptive modification is a tension felt by both curriculum developers and teachers. Some materials have been developed with the intent that teachers would use them exactly as they were written with no modifications or variations. Other materials acknowledge the need for local adaptation and are designed to encourage variation. More recently, the recognition that teaching is an ongoing process of design and that teachers must interpret teaching materials and resources for their classrooms and students has begun to influence curriculum developers (Brown and Edelson 2003). Teacher modification of curriculum materials is discussed in greater detail later in the chapter.

> "Teachers' interpretations of the design and features of innovative materials are greatly influenced by their own backgrounds, knowledge, and skills."

Teachers' Use of Texts

The use of newer, innovative materials is varied at the high school level, due to the ways teachers have traditionally used textbooks. Those who use textbooks as flexible resources of information and activities often believe that carefully designed, research-based instructional materials can be similarly used. Ball and Cohen (1996) found that when high school teachers were presented with a set of designed instructional materials, they tended to use only pieces of those materials or adapt them or integrate them without understanding the grand scheme of how the learning activities were designed to be sequenced, meshed, or taught.

This observation was reinforced in a CSE study (EDC 2001) investigating how teachers used several research-based curricula. Researchers found a striking difference between the intentions of the developers (the intended curriculum) and the actual implementation by teachers in the classroom (the enacted curriculum).

During the first year of using these materials, most teachers implemented the materials with a high degree of fidelity; however, with each year of use, teacher adaptations and modifications of the materials increased significantly.

Ball and Cohen attributed the uneven role of innovative curricula in science education reform to several factors, including (a) curriculum developers' failure to appreciate teachers' need to learn how to use the new materials; (b) teachers' views that designed curricular materials constrain and control their role as creative designers of their own materials; and (c) teachers' own beliefs about what constitutes effective teaching, the needs of their students, and the external demands of school policy, parents, and testing.

Other factors may also contribute to difficulties in implementing innovative curricular materials. Many teachers feel that the inquiry approach advocated by most of these curricula is time-consuming and that the content demands of their state frameworks require more direct instruction. Complex scheduling issues and interruptions put additional constraints on the time teachers feel they can spend on the implementation of an inquiry approach. In addition, authentic assessments that often accompany these materials require much more time to grade than short-answer, multiple-choice tests. Perhaps the biggest factor is the failure of curriculum developers to accommodate the needs and roles of teachers in the materials.

Teachers as Curriculum Designers

The art of teaching is an ongoing process of curriculum design. For many teachers, a textbook or curriculum serves as the starting point or resource for customizing the materials for each specific classroom. In her book, *The Teacher-Curriculum Encounter: Freeing Teachers From the Tyranny of Texts*, Miriam Ben-Peretz (1990) described teachers as interpreters of "curriculum potential." She defined curriculum potential as the interaction of two elements—the materials themselves (the intended curriculum) and the use of the materials based on the teacher interpretation (the enacted curriculum). The enacted curriculum may result in a broader application of the materials than the developer envisioned, but also may result in instruction that fails to reflect the developers' original intentions and, therefore, fails to incorporate new teaching practices that form an integral part of the curriculum design.

The interpretations of a designed curriculum are the result of the many factors teachers bring to bear in their teaching. These factors include the depth of their own content knowledge, their choices about what content is important to know based on their own interests and requirements of their district and state, their beliefs about the nature of good teaching and learning, their comfort level with different instructional strategies, their recognition of the diverse needs of their students, and a desire to make learning relevant to the experiences of their students (site-based learning). Modifications and adaptations of curricula may then be the result of how teachers choose to use the curricular materials to meet their needs and the needs of their students.

Ben-Peretz (1990) suggested that before a curriculum can reach its full educational potential, curriculum developers must recognize the *teacher dimension*.

Innovative Curricula as Professional Development

When developers do not explain their rationale for constructing the materials in a certain way, teachers may unknowingly undermine the curriculum's intent (Ben-Peretz 1990). For example, developers may present a more sociological framework in order to motivate students to learn through a real-life lens. Or developers may present concepts in an unfamiliar sequence because research has suggested that students learn better when concepts are built slowly and are connected to ideas that went before and ideas to come. Without understanding why certain decisions were made by the developers, teachers may interpret the materials in ways that run counter to the intentions of the developers and to the overall integrity of the curriculum.

Recently, great interest has turned to the role of curricula in providing opportunities for teacher learning. Opportunities for teachers to learn new ways of teaching and making instructional decisions as they teach have been embedded in the instructional materials. As defined by Davis and Krajcik (2005), teacher learning can result when teachers receive guidance in applying their content knowledge, along with their knowledge about teaching and learning, to their instructional decisions. Davis and Krajcik have developed nine design heuristics focused on a teacher's knowledge base relating to both subject-matter knowledge and pedagogical content knowledge. These heuristics are designed to guide curriculum developers as they incorporate such supports into their materials. Development of curricula that is both educative and transparent in rationale and intentions can support teachers in developing what Brown and Edelson (2003) call "pedagogical design capacity." Pedagogical design capacity is the ability to perceive and use innovative curricula as a basis for customizing instruction to the specific needs of teachers and their students while retaining developer intent.

Although the specific concepts of educative curricula are only now being precisely identified by education researchers, EDC has long held the philosophy that making the developers' intentions transparent to the teacher for both content and teaching is essential in supporting the implementation of the materials. Two EDC-developed high school curricula, *Insights in Biology*, an introductory biology curriculum, and *Foundation Science*, a comprehensive program encompassing all disciplines for grades 9 through 12, reflect this perspective.

The major components of these curricula include a student book that contains the readings and activities forming the core of the learning and a teacher's guide containing supports for implementing the materials and for understanding the design of the materials. The teacher's guide contains features designed to promote teacher learning and acquisition of new teaching practices:

* An introductory section at the beginning of each volume that discusses the content that is addressed, ways the content is sequenced and why, the teaching and learning principles employed, different instructional strategies, the roles and uses of formative and summative assessments, and practical considerations for implementing the instructional materials
* Identification of the understanding goals, assessment outcomes, possible misconceptions, and assumptions of prior knowledge and skills at the beginning of each learning experience
* Overviews of each learning experience linking the concepts students are about to explore with those the students have already learned
* A description of the purpose and intended outcome of each section, activity, reading, and discussion within a learning experience
* Teaching strategies designed to give teachers support in (a) using students' prior knowledge and addressing misconceptions; (b) using alternative ways to address a concept and carry out an activity and to make connections to previous understandings; (c) helping students to construct meaning from their activities, readings, and discussions; and (d) assisting students to keep track of their ideas and thinking
* Supports for facilitating activities, including things to watch for, troubleshooting an experiment, methods for helping students move through the activity or design an investigation, suggestions for helping students with data collection and analysis, and alternative ways to carry out the steps in the activity
* Guidance in helping students interpret their data and use evidence and scientific understandings to support their conclusions
* Supports for facilitating discussions, including sample questions and possible responses and strategies for encouraging student discussion
* Explanations of the tools for determining student learning, such as questions to help determine student understanding (listening for understanding), embedded assessments, end-of-unit assessments, and assessment item banks
* Scientific background that provides information on recent scientific findings and deepens and expands teacher content knowledge beyond the level of student understanding to facilitate explanations of scientific concepts

The goal of these features is to help teachers implement the materials, understand the intention of the developers, and incorporate new approaches into their teaching. The outcome of these educative components is that the teacher can adapt and modify the materials while retaining the philosophical, conceptual, and pedagogical approaches intended by the materials.

Having explored the principles of innovative curricula and the teacher's role in employing the curricula, let's take another look at Theresa, the chemistry teacher in the earlier vignette and at her experience with the new curriculum.

Theresa has been using the new chemistry curriculum for a year and a half now. As agreed, she tried to teach the materials as written for the first year. Several things about the curriculum, however, baffled her. She didn't understand the rationale for the sequence of lessons and for the inclusion of certain content. Also, she was inexperienced with some of the instructional strategies suggested, such as role-playing and presentations.

Furthermore, Theresa was worried about the time she would have to spend introducing her students to the real-life situation (or "context") for each lesson. For example, the lesson on chemical change used this situation: The copper on the Statue of Liberty, which had originally been extracted from ore, has turned green over the years. *Students were to gather background information on the building of the statue. Then, they moved to the lesson's "challenge"—in this case, they were to propose an approach for restoring the copper burnish to the statue. For her students to be able to address this "challenge" they needed to gather information. They conducted an investigation in which they isolated copper from ore and read about chemical reactions, including the oxidation of copper. They then used the understandings gained from the investigation and the reading to propose a solution to the problem. This approach took more time than having the students just read about chemical change and then discuss the topic in class. However, she stuck with it.*

As the year progressed, Theresa began to make new conceptual connections and to understand why the developers spent extended time on content that she did not normally focus on. She also observed a new buzz in the classroom as students became engaged in the real-life situations that had been created for each lesson.

However, Theresa also saw places in the curriculum where she wanted to make modifications and adaptations based on the needs of her students and her interest as a content expert. For example, she wanted to make the real-life situations that framed the lessons more relevant to her own students. She decided to use a local event as the context for investigating physical properties and change. A hurricane had recently battered the coastal town in which the students lived. The oil refinery, which was the town's major industry and employer, had been particularly hard-hit: The crude oil in the refinery had been contaminated with seawater and sand. Using this real-life situation, the students were challenged to apply their understandings about physical properties and change to design an efficient method to (a) remove the salt water and sand contaminants and then (b) separate the crude oil into its individual components.

It had been a tough year for Theresa. Learning to use the materials wasn't easy, especially after years of designing her own curricula. In the end, though, Theresa decided it was worth it. The new curriculum had given her insights into teaching and learning and a structured approach to the content she needed to teach. It also gave her the flexibility she required as a professional with years of experience.

Theresa felt she would continue to learn from the new curriculum while adapting it to meet her own teaching goals and the needs of her students. For example, she felt her students needed more math, and she identified appropriate places in the new curriculum where she could incorporate mathematical applications She also decided to stick with the role-playing and presentations. Although they took a lot of time, she found that they were good ways for students to enhance their communication skills and to synthesize what they were doing in each learning experience.

Conclusion

This chapter has examined the interplay between the intended implementation of designed, innovative instructional materials and the enacted curriculum by teachers who are accustomed to customizing their own instruction. When EDC began its studies of implementation fidelity (EDC 2001), it was assumed that teachers would use the materials as the developers intended. The goal of the study was to find out how, in reality, teachers used them. The findings were eye opening but not surprising. Teachers modified, supplemented, and rearranged the materials according to their own beliefs about good teaching and learning and in response to the needs of their students.

Teachers' use of curriculum as a resource for their own design is not only an inevitability but a critical and necessary component of good teaching. As education researcher Lee Shulman stated, "In principle, no curriculum is adequate because it cannot anticipate the infinite variation of teachers, students, and contexts…. The essential value of curriculum is how it permits teachers to adapt, invent, and transform it as they confront the realities of the classroom" (Ben-Peretz 1990, Introduction).

In recent years, several groups have begun to research the impact of implementation fidelity on student learning. It may be incumbent upon researchers also to better define implementation fidelity in the classroom and to acknowledge that teachers must make adaptations in designed curricula. The challenge for developers of an innovative curriculum is to improve support and guidance for teachers as they make it their own while maintaining its nuanced conceptual and pedagogical foundations. If the curriculum truly supports teacher learning, the enacted curriculum may vary widely from classroom to classroom but will retain its pedagogical essence and intended spirit.

Recommended Resources

AAAS Project 2061 High School Science Textbook Evaluations. Ten biology textbooks are measured for their utility in helping students learn skills as outlined in *Benchmarks for Science Literacy* and in *National Science Education Standards. www.project2061.org/about/press/pr000627. htm#books*

BSCS Profiles in Science (Biological Sciences Curriculum Study). This report on 17 reform programs devised by the National Science Foundation includes descriptions of programs. *www. bscs.org/page.asp?pageid=0|124|185|184&id=0|profiles*

Guiding Middle Grade Curriculum Decisions (Center for Science Education, Education Development Center, Inc). Selected exemplary curriculum middle school programs are profiled in this reference guide. The report also includes strategies for making curriculum decisions. *www.middleweb.com/EDC/EDCmain.html*

Review of Biological Institute Materials for Secondary Schools (American Institute of Biological Science). This consumer-report-style review of widely used secondary biology texts assesses the materials' quality, scientific accuracy, teaching strategies, and teacher support. *www. aibs.org/books/resources/TextbookReview.pdf*

Review of Evaluation Studies of Mathematics and Science Curricula and Professional Development Models (The Urban Institute). This report uses increases in student achievement to rate the effectiveness of middle and high school science. *www.urban.org/url.cfm?ID=311150*

Selected Standard-Based Curriculum Profiles (Center for Science Education, Education Development Center, Inc.). These profiles contain brief descriptions of exemplary and promising K-12 science curricula. *http://cse.edc.org/pdfs/curriculum/10currprof.pdf*

LEADERSHIP
IN SCIENCE
EDUCATION REFORM

Building Leadership Teams to Create Professional Learning Communities in Secondary Schools

Jody Bintz and Nancy Landes
Biological Sciences Curriculum Study (BSCS)

"The winners of the next decade and beyond will be those who can build people and build teams." —Thomas Harvey and Bonita Drolet (1994)

Because teaching and learning are inextricably linked, student performance will not likely increase without transformations in teaching. Through teamwork, school and district personnel can develop a common vision of teaching and learning. Through teamwork, teachers can develop greater understanding of the work of their colleagues within their grade or course and across grades and courses. Through teamwork, teachers and administrators can learn to build trust and cultivate shared leadership in the work of improving science teaching and learning. Through teamwork, an entire school staff can become a professional learning community, and only through teamwork can we hope to reform science education.

According to DuFour and Eaker (1998), "The most promising strategy for sustained, substantive school improvement is developing the ability of school personnel to function as professional learning communities" (p. xi). Our own experience tells us that building leadership teams is an essential step toward creating such professional learning communities in secondary schools.

Teamwork does not occur without vision, planning, and effort. A leadership team can transform the traditional, isolated landscape of secondary schools into communities of learners where teaming is the norm. To begin thinking about establishing a leadership team to guide reform, you should consider the following five questions:

1. Why work together?
2. Who will be on our leadership team?
3. How will we work together?
4. When and where will we meet?
5. What will be our shared work?

As Garmston and Wellman (1999) attested, expert teams are made, not born. The next few pages will provide answers to these five questions and showcase the important lessons we have learned from the work of BSCS (Biological Sciences Curriculum Study) through the National Academy for Curriculum Leadership (NACL). NACL is a three-year professional development program developed in collaboration with WestEd and with funding from the National Science Foundation.

Key Question 1: Why work together?
Lesson Learned: Effective teams can lead to dynamic professional learning communities.
Professional learning communities create a collective sense of responsibility for student learning and form the cornerstone for sustainable science reform. A school-based leadership team can be the seed of a professional learning community. An effective leadership team embodies the characteristics of a professional learning community with shared norms and values, a focus on student learning, collaboration, deprivatized practice, and reflective dialogue (see Figure 5.1). The members of the leadership team learn together how to exhibit these characteristics as they work collaboratively. In turn, they plan for the professional learning of their colleagues so that the concept of professional learning community becomes concrete. The leadership team is a viable means to the end of sustainable science reform through the development of a professional learning community within the school or district.

Figure 5.1

Five characteristics of a professional learning community

Shared norms and values
Shared norms and values form the foundation for all aspects of developing a professional learning community. Teachers and administrators must reinforce their own understandings about children and learning, teaching and teachers' roles, and the nature of human needs, activities, and relationships.

A focus on student learning
Most curricular programs in schools emphasize gaining new techniques, skills, and delivery strategies over monitoring the connections between the use of new practices and a focus on student learning. Professional learning communities place sustained attention on students, thereby emphasizing how pedagogy is linked to the process of student learning.

Collaboration
Collegial relations are characterized by mutual learning that comes from joint planning of future teaching activities and improved learning support. Collaboration is the most advanced form of collegiality. Genuine collaboration involves the codevelopment of skills related to new practice and the generation of knowledge, ideas, and programs that advance expertise and school performance.

Deprivatized practice
Deprivatized practice means that teachers practice their craft openly through sharing their knowledge and skills with one another. Sometimes, this sharing takes the form of peer mentoring, sharing through lesson study, examining student work, or another strategy that brings about communication and collaboration. In much of this work, teachers bring real teaching problems to colleagues, thus promoting practice that is no longer private.

Reflective dialogue
Reflective dialogue is key to professional learning communities because it encourages self-awareness about practice. As teachers and administrators engage in reflective dialogue, they close the gap between theory and practice, reduce isolation, and become students of teaching and learning.

Source: Louis, K. S., and S.D. Kruse. 1995. *Professionalism and community: Perspectives on reforming urban schools.* Thousand Oaks, CA: Corwin Press.

Key Question 2: Who will be on our leadership team?
Lesson Learned: The structure and composition of the team matter.

Forming a leadership team requires planning, especially in the following areas:

* The way the school or district will prepare for the creation of a leadership team
* The nature of the relationship between this leadership team and other teams or committees already in existence
* The members of the leadership team
* The individual(s) who will determine the composition of the leadership team, how this decision will be made, and the criteria on which the decision will be based
* The individual and collective roles and responsibilities of the team members

Creating readiness for the formation of a leadership team includes developing awareness of the reform effort within the school or district science community, whether the reform is about implementing new instructional materials, strengthening inquiry-based teaching strategies, or applying formative classroom assessment techniques. Developing criteria for membership and sharing roles and responsibilities is a critical early step in the process. Lambert (2003) recommended using criteria identified by the faculty to select team members. In our experience with the NACL, schools and districts have selected team members based on their ability to help lead the work that needed to be accomplished.

In the work of secondary science reform, we have found that the ideal leadership team is composed of four to seven members and includes a key administrator, teachers, and possibly a supporting member from the school district or community (see Figure 5.2). The teachers recruited to the team might be existing leaders or teachers who have leadership potential. The key administrator provides the team with administrative support and access to district resources.

Figure 5.2

National Academy for Curriculum Leadership (NACL) leadership team members

* **A key administrator:** science supervisor, district curriculum coordinator, building principal, assistant principal, or science department chairperson with budget authority
* **Two or more science teachers:** current classroom teachers involved in the focus of the science reform, such as the implementation of new instructional materials or new instructional practices
* **A district or community supporter:** could be a school board member, a consultant, retired teacher, preservice teacher educator, or member of the business community recruited to support the team's efforts
* **A coach:** teacher or supporter selected from among the team members to facilitate and guide the team as it works together to become more reflective about adult learning and the change process

As part of our work with NACL teams, we have instituted the role of "coach" on the team. The coach is either a teacher leader or the district or community supporter. To enhance opportunities for shared leadership, the key administrator does not serve in the role of coach, but rather supports the coach and participates as a team member, albeit one with authority (Garmston and Wellman 1999). We found the role of coach to be critical to the success of the leadership team.

Primary concerns cited by new leadership team members we have worked with include their role on the team, their responsibilities in the reform effort, and the fit of their work within the existing goals of the school or district. These types of personal concerns are to be expected. (See Chapter 2 for an explanation of Stages of Concern.) Coaches and key administrators help individuals grow into their leadership roles, make sense of the work, and assume the responsibilities associated with implementing new instructional materials or practices.

Key Question 3: How will we work together?
Lesson Learned: Teams need to attend to team development and communication.

For teams to grow and develop, team members need to "have conversations about 'how to do the work' instead of just plunging in to do the work. They need to spend time building trust and relationships with each other" (Richardson 2005, p. 3). Trust is needed so that team members can have the difficult conversations required to effect change. They must also develop the knowledge and skills supporting effective communication.

The conversations about both what work needs to be done and how to do the work often begin in team meetings. Harvey (1995) recommends that the first team meeting have no task goal; rather, it should be devoted to team building and getting to know one another. Then, as the team moves into building agendas and accomplishing tasks, the members should always include time for reflecting on their teamwork and developing themselves as a team.

Garmston and Wellman (1999) recommended that newly formed teams "devote 50% of their time to tasks and 50% of their time to learning, monitoring, and strengthening processes" (p. 64). As teams progress, they adjust the ratio of time spent on task and process. A rule of thumb for meetings of 90 minutes or less is to commit about 15 minutes to monitoring and reflecting on process. According to Harvey and Drolet (1994, p. 11), "team-building cannot be a one-time event, something you do in September or January with the hope it will last throughout the year." Teams must attend to team development on an ongoing basis.

The NACL team's coach, supported by the key administrator, plays a critical role in helping the whole team develop the requisite knowledge, skills, and abilities to become an effective team. The coach supports and challenges the team, often calls meetings, and helps focus the team's work. The coach pays attention to both the outcomes of the work and the processes used to achieve the outcomes. The coach often collaborates with the key administrator to set meeting agendas and works behind the scenes to make sure the tasks established by the team are accomplished. The coach promotes shared leadership among team members. One concrete example of shared leadership is rotating the role of facilitator during team meetings.

To successfully fill the role, coaches must have or develop facilitation skills and, in turn, help team members develop their capacity to facilitate the team. These skills include assisting the team (a) to set, observe, and reflect on norms and guidelines for how the team will work together; (b) to identify opportunities for dialogue (conversation focused on developing greater understanding of ideas) and discussion (conversation focused on making a decision); and (c) to clarify the decision-making process and the team's role in making decisions.

a. Norms and guidelines. Members of productive teams establish norms or ground rules and hold themselves and one another accountable to them. Examples of ground rules commonly used by teams include

* using an agenda,
* beginning and ending on time,
* balancing participation, and
* engaging conflict positively (e.g., struggling together about ideas, not people).

Although these guidelines or ground rules are important reminders to help team members work together, they do not provide team members with the knowledge and skills to communicate effectively during their meetings. Garmston and Wellman (1999) established the Seven Norms of Collaboration to help leadership teams develop a common set of behaviors and skills to promote dialogue, thus laying the foundation for better decision making (see Figure 5.3).

Figure 5.3

Seven norms of collaborative work

Pausing: Pausing before responding or asking a question allows time for thinking and enhances dialogue, discussion, and decision making.

Paraphrasing: Using a paraphrase starter that is comfortable for you—e.g., "So..." or "As you are saying..." or "You're thinking..." —and then following the starter with a paraphrase helps members of the group hear and understand each other as they formulate decisions.

Probing: Using gentle, open-ended probes or inquiries such as, "Please say more..." or "I'm curious about..." or "I'd like to hear more about..." or "Then are you saying...?" increases the clarity and precision of the group's thinking.

Putting ideas on the table: Ideas are the heart of a meaningful dialogue. Label the intention of your comments; for example, you might say, "Here is one idea..." or "One thought I have is..." or "Here is a possible approach...."

Paying attention to self and others: Meaningful dialogue is facilitated when each group member is conscious of him- or herself and of others and is aware of not only what he or she is saying, but also how it is said and how others are responding. This includes paying attention to learning styles when planning for, facilitating, and participating in group meetings. Responding to others in their own language is one manifestation of this norm.

Presuming positive intentions: Assuming that the intentions of others are positive promotes and facilitates meaningful dialogue and eliminates unintentional put-downs. Using positive intentions in your speech is one manifestation of this norm.

Pursuing a balance between advocacy and inquiry: Pursuing and maintaining a balance between advocating a position and inquiring about one's own and others' positions assists the group in becoming a learning organization.

Source: Garmston, R. J., and B. M. Wellman. 1999. *The adaptive school: A sourcebook for developing collaborative groups.* Norwood, MA: Christopher-Gordon Publishers.

Individual team members begin to build the skills to develop a highly effective team by paying attention to and practicing the skills and behaviors implicit in the Norms of Collaboration. These norms provide common language so that individuals can reflect on their personal use of the norms as well as on how the team as a whole is doing.

b. Dialogue and discussion. Dialogue and discussion are two different ways of talking. In dialogue, the purpose of the conversation is to develop a clear understanding of ideas among the participants. The purpose of a discussion is to talk in ways that lead to a decision. Whether in dialogue or discussion, the Norms of Collaboration provide a valuable guide for communication. When pursuing a conversation consistent with dialogue, team members focus on using the norms of paraphrasing, probing, and inquiring, while a discussion would add the layer of advocating for one's ideas or the ideas of others.

In a meeting, teams designate and use specific strategies that support dialogue prior to making important decisions. Strategies are chosen much as a teacher selects an instructional strategy. The strategy may be as simple as identifying a specified time for dialogue prior to discussion as part of the agenda or as complex as publicly recording ideas from the group, clarifying the ideas generated, advocating among ideas, and reaching consensus about which ideas to pursue. Recording and clarifying ideas is more consistent with dialogue, while advocating and reaching consensus is more consistent with discussion.

Structuring meetings around dialogue and discussion requires planning not only in the selection of the strategy, but also in sharing roles such as facilitator, timekeeper, and recorder as part of using the strategy. The responsibility for planning may be shared, but the implementation of the strategy requires leadership from the coach and, likely, from the key administrator.

c. Decision making. A clearly defined process for making a decision, described as part of a discussion in the previous section, helps teams become efficient and effective. The process may involve a vote, consensus building, a decision made by an individual with or without input, or a unilateral decision made by an individual or another group (Garmston and Wellman 1999).

Trust is key to building an effective team. Trust is put at risk when the team is unclear about the level of decision-making authority within the team or the process that will be used in making a decision. Teams must be clear about whether they are providing information, making a recommendation to others who will then make the decision, or making the decision themselves. If there are limits to the decision that may be made, the limits (or at a minimum, the potential existence of limits) need to be clearly communicated.

Key Question 4: When and where will we meet?
Lesson Learned: Team development takes time and persistence.

Teams can become highly effective over time. They need opportunities to meet and work together, which requires a commitment of time and other resources, as well as a plan for productive use of these valuable resources. The coach and, likely, the key administrator take on the initial responsibility for scheduling meetings and planning agendas; however, as the team develops, these tasks may be shared among team members.

The key question of when and where to meet suggests that teams need to pay attention to the small details of teamwork, as well as to the larger issues of communicating and building trust. Generally, teams set regular meeting schedules—for example, once or twice a month—in a location that is "neutral" territory, that is, a place where they can meet in comfort but attend to the business at hand without distractions. Teams take the time to get together on a regular basis and value the time they have together.

As teams establish their routines about when and where to meet, and as team members learn more about one another and pay attention to how they are working together, the meetings gradually change. According to psychologist Bruce Tuckman (1965), as teams pay attention to their development over time, they often move among various predictable stages that include forming, storming, norming, and performing

Figure 5.4

Stages of team development

New Group "Forming"	Divided Group "Storming"	Equitable Team "Norming"	Highly Effective Team "Performing"
Dependence on coach	Question/challenge role of coach	Balanced roles	High level of productivity
Unclear about tasks	No sense of potency/success	Clear about tasks	Synergistic
Unclear about purpose of team	No flow of information	Group cohesiveness	Attention to group maintenance
Unclear about roles	Formation of independent factions	Mutual trust	Interdependent
Low level of productivity	Roles not balanced	Common identity	Healthy stress
Group process minimal to nonexistent	Low level of productivity	Consistent flow of information	Conflict management
	Unclear method for making decisions	Collaboration in decision making	Norms of collaboration
		Open conflict	Shared leadership
		Effective questioning/ listening	Apprehension about the end of the team's work together

(see Figure 5.4). These stages are a normal part of team development and are important for teams to experience before they can become highly effective.

Recognizing the developmental nature of team growth may be as important as understanding the stages. Knowing that team members are typically unclear about roles and that storming (the stage in which different ideas compete for consideration) can be expected is comforting—the predictability provides a level of control. With awareness and understanding, teams can make decisions that help them continue to become more effective.

Various phenomena may cause an existing team to move among the stages. These phenomena can be expected to impact the team as a whole, as well as individual team members. For example, teams may add or lose members or the context in which the team is working may change. In these instances, teams can expect to exhibit characteristics more consistent with the forming or storming stage. In addition, as teams with consistent membership reach the performing level, a return to forming and storming is sometimes desirable, necessary, and logical in order to maintain energy and focus on reform. The stages are often cyclical, especially as team tasks and responsibilities become more complex.

Key Question 5: What will be our shared work?
Lesson Learned: Effective teams develop by learning together and working together to effect change.
"Team learning is not 'team building' and should not be taken lightly" (Senge et al. 1994). Teams are effective only when they are engaged in meaningful tasks. As teams work together, they learn about and use processes and tools (see Table 5.1 for examples) that require them to engage in conversations about their own work as school or district leaders and about the real work of classroom teachers and students. These tools and processes provide leadership teams with opportunities to demonstrate the characteristics of a professional learning community. In turn, members of the leadership teams support the use of these tools and processes in the broader school and district community, providing opportunities for all science teachers to engage as a professional learning community.

Table 5.1 shows the links between areas of shared work in which the NACL leadership teams were involved and specific characteristics of a professional learning community. These areas of shared work provide the basis of professional development activities for the leadership team and the school or district staff. The activities are structured to advance the development of a professional learning community at the building level and to provide the types of learning opportunities and the tools that help move school or district science reform efforts forward.

While the leadership team learns about and uses the tools and processes of their shared work, such as data-driven dialogue, team members also engage in the use of specific tools and processes that support team development, such as the Norms of Collaboration. Periodically, the team members should pause and reflect on how they are doing with specific norms. During this time, individuals might share specific things they have done to honor the norm or ways another team member has helped the team practice the norm.

The key to this final lesson learned is twofold: (1) A leadership team develops through doing work that is important to the school or district, and (2) the development of a leadership team means nothing in the end if it does not have an impact on teacher practice and student learning. Leadership teams need resources, including professional development, to build the capacity of individual team members and to build the capacity of the team as a whole. Such attention to team development will help lead to an effective science reform effort and promote teamwork as part of a strong, vibrant professional learning community in a school and district.

Closing Thoughts

This chapter proposes one way to foster teamwork and develop a professional learning community at the secondary level by describing the development of a leadership team focused on improving science teaching and learning. Forming

Table 5.1

The shared work supporting the development of a professional learning community (PLC)

Understanding, Tool, or Process for Leadership Teams and Teachers in the School/District	Related Characteristic of a PLC
Science as Inquiry Participants engage in personal learning experiences that contribute to the development of a common vision for teaching and learning through inquiry. (See Chapters 1 and 2 for examples.)	Shared Norms and Values Collaboration
Analyzing Instructional Materials (AIM) Participants use this evidence-based, collaborative process for analyzing instructional materials using standards and research-based criteria. (See Chapter 3 for an overview of the process.)	Shared Norms and Values Collaboration
Examining Student Work and Collaborative Lesson Study Participants use collaborative processes to examine student work and to co-plan lessons that engage them in rich conversations that are close to the real work of teachers and students.	Focus on Student Learning Deprivatized Practice Reflective Dialogue
Data-Driven Dialogue Participants use data-driven dialogue (Love 2002) as a process for analyzing student learning data that includes publicly displaying predictions, observations, and inferences about the data and a method for asking questions about where the observations and inferences might lead. (See Chapter 7 for examples.)	Focus on Student Learning Collaboration Deprivatized Practice Reflective Dialogue
Concerns-Based Adoption Model Leadership teams use the Concerns-Based Adoption Model to clarify their work, determine teacher concerns, and assess levels of implementation. (See Chapter 2 for more details and examples.)	Shared Norms and Values Collaboration Reflective Dialogue
Professional Development Design Leadership teams learn about and use the Design Framework for Professional Development (Loucks-Horsley et al. 2003) as a way of understanding the change process and monitoring progress while planning an effective professional development program.	Collaboration Reflective Dialogue

Source: Based on the authors' work in the National Academy for Curriculum Leadership.

a leadership team is just the first step. We often expect a team of adults to know *how* to work together; however, we find that this is a false assumption. Our hope is that this chapter has provided ideas and insights into how to build a team as part of the task of improving science teaching and learning, as well as how to help the team and the entire school community develop the skills and abilities to work together as a true professional learning community.

How might you accept the challenge as a leader in science education to contribute to the development of an effective leadership team to improve science teaching and learning in your district or school? What have the five lessons learned meant to you? How will you use what you have learned to further your own work in reforming science education in your school or district?

How you answer these questions will have a profound effect on the efforts to reform secondary science education and to promote the learning of science for all.

Recommended Resources

Blythe, T., D. Allen, and B. Scheiffelin. 2007. *Looking together at student work.* New York: Teachers College Press. A practical guide to collaborative examination of student work to improve instruction.

DuFour, R., and R. Eaker. 1998. *Professional learning communities at work: Best practices for enhancing student achievement.* Bloomington, IN: National Education Service. Tips on how to build professional communities that focus on school improvement.

Garmston, R. J., and B. M. Wellman. 1999. *The adaptive school: A sourcebook for developing collaborative groups.* Norwood, MA: Christopher-Gordon Publishers. A must-have resource for advice on building professional communities, developing collaborative norms, facilitating meetings, and working toward school change.

Love, N. 2002. *Using data/getting results: A practical guide to school improvement in mathematics and science with CD-ROM.* Norwood, MA: Christopher-Gordon Publishers. A how-to resource manual describing school-based data collection and analysis to inform change in curriculum, instruction, and assessment practices.

6

Essential Partnerships in the Reform of Secondary Science

Julie A. Luft
Arizona State University

The chief difficulty Alice found at first was in managing her flamingo: she suc-
ceeded in getting its body tucked away, comfortably enough, under her arm, with
its legs hanging down, but generally, just as she had got its neck nicely straight-
ened out…it WOULD twist itself round and look up in her face, with such a
puzzled expression that she could not help bursting out laughing…. Alice soon
came to the conclusion that it was a very difficult game indeed.[1]

Alice's travel through Wonderland resembles our journeys with reform. We often encounter new experiences. We learn from events. Some tasks are harder to complete than they initially appear. Moreover, we tend to encounter the same lively characters in our reform efforts that Alice encountered in her journey. There are people who constantly give us direction, people who make quick decisions, and people who listen and ask good questions. This short list can easily be expanded to include everyone involved in reform efforts. The list is not as important, however, as realizing that these different participants are important in our journey if we are going to arrive at our final destination. In the case of Alice, she was transformed from a young child to a young adult, and in our case we are moving toward environments that foster improved student learning.

If we are to engage successfully in reform efforts, we must work effectively with those who are part of our journey. This group may include science teach-

---

[1] All quotations are from Lewis Carroll's *Alice in Wonderland.*

ers, students, administrators, science and education faculty, businesses, and parents. Our collective strengths are greater than the strength of any individual. No individual can successfully develop and implement reform in the schools without seeking help from others who may be participants in change (Hall and Hord 2001). Accomplishing such a feat requires us to adopt a set of guiding principles for building and coordinating our partnership. With these simple principles, we can create an environment that allows us to work together while solving the simple and complex problems found in reform projects (Sirotnik and Goodlad 1988).

In this chapter, we will address the different aspects of building partnerships to support reform efforts. Our intention is to provide new insights into the importance of collaborative efforts and guidance in facilitating productive partnerships.

Types of Partnerships

"Now we have seen each other," said the Unicorn. "If you'll believe in me, I'll believe in you. Is that a bargain?"

Partnerships, as discussed by Smedley (2001), provide an enhanced role for practitioners, new avenues to collaborations for academics and business leaders, and involvement opportunities for parents. They also form an evolving group that is the catalyst for change. Schools with these types of partnerships enjoy an ongoing examination of student learning from different perspectives and a dynamic dialogue focused on enhancing the learning of all participants. This type of configuration clearly requires the combined strengths of teachers, administrators, faculty members, parents, and business leaders, as each has skills and abilities critical to the educational process.

A variety of partnerships can occur in reform programs. For instance, businesses can participate in the development of science education programs by providing resources and experts in areas not typically found in schools. Community leaders can participate in reform by revealing the complexity of learning in a specific culture. Parents can partner in reform programs by working closely with teachers to support student learning. School personnel, who are the center of reform programs, bring a comprehensive knowledge base about schools, learning, teaching, and students. All of these individuals can contribute to the partnership. Moreover, a focus on student learning provides each member with the opportunity to contribute to and receive from the reform effort.

Who Can Be a Partner?

The Caterpillar and Alice looked at each other for some time in silence … and [the Caterpillar] addressed her in a languid, sleepy voice.
"Who are YOU?" said the Caterpillar.

Potential partners do not look like one another, nor do they bring the same resources or skills to the partnership. Instead, as in Alice's journey, partnerships in reform are composed of people who have varying skills and resources. For instance, some people are more highly skilled at working with students while others have a stronger knowledg of science content. They may also have varying levels of appreciation for the complexity of teaching science. Yet even with these differences there is at least one common desire—impacting and improving the learning of students. "Student learning must be viewed as the primary purpose of schooling," say the National Science Education Standards (NRC 1996, p. 232).

In order to depict the potential of a partnership in a science education reform effort, we will describe one reform effort. The Districtwide Emphasis on Science Education Reform in Tucson (DESERT) was a local systemic initiative lasting for six years in southern Arizona. It entailed the development of a partnership between a school district and a university, with the goal of infusing science as inquiry into the schools. In the College of Science of this university, scientists became involved when they realized that graduate students in science needed opportunities to work in secondary school settings. Science faculty members were concerned that their graduate students would ultimately pursue careers requiring some experience in working with teachers and schools. For the university scientists, this seemed like the perfect opportunity for their students to gain this experience—while they were in school and prior to employment.

Ultimately, the scientists developed a program in which science graduate students served as substitute science teachers, while science teachers participated in professional development programs. In this program, the graduate students taught a lesson from the adopted science curriculum to ensure that science concepts were covered during the teacher's absence. In addition to having a knowledgeable substitute, the teachers were able to leave their classes for a few hours, as opposed to an entire day. It was an ideal partnership for both the teachers and the graduate students: Teachers could participate in professional development programs during the school day, and science graduate students learned about middle school science classrooms.

In the College of Education, another type of partnership was developed. Faculty members and their graduate students in science education, who were interested in various aspects of reform and wanted to study site-based professional development programs, became involved in the evaluation of the program. The opportunity for the graduate students to participate in studies of schools in the midst of change could not be surpassed. Likewise, the staff needed information about the project at the school level, and it allowed them to modify their program accordingly.

Building Partnerships

"Begin at the beginning," the King said, gravely, "and go on till you come to the end: then stop."

Partnerships are formed for many reasons. Some partnerships are formed to develop new curriculum, while others are convened to support a new instructional model. Even though these partnerships are developed in response to different goals, they should have four qualities in common: They should be need-based, have clear goals, have appropriate complexity, and be sound, practical programs (Fullan 2001). In the following paragraphs, we elaborate on these qualities in the context of the DESERT project.

Responds to a Need

The partnership should be formed in response to a *need*. In terms of science instruction, needs can include improving the curriculum, connecting to local issues, enhancing the quantity and quality of science instruction, moving from a textbook to hands-on science, or developing science leadership capacity in a school or district. In all cases, improved student learning should ultimately be supported.

The DESERT project was developed in response to the extensive use of textbooks in the science classroom, which did not contribute to students engaging in science as inquiry. Once under way, this project helped teachers build their content and pedagogical knowledge so they could use the district science curriculum, which was kit based, to impact student learning through hands-on science experiences. Thus, the DESERT program was formed to address the need to provide students with rich science experiences.

Clear Goals and Sufficient Means

Once a partnership is formed, *clear goals* and *the means* to accomplish these goals should be identified. Clear goals are essential in depicting the outcome of the partnership. In the DESERT project, the goal of developing leadership capacity at the middle school science level was specified, with the intention of supporting teachers as they use more hands-on materials. The design of the program was based on the development of leaders through various experiences in science with district curriculum and through a process of lesson study.

These clearly stated goals allowed project partners to identify the areas in which they could contribute to the project. In addition, the goals allowed the partners to articulate the means by which they were to be accomplished. As the district and university contributed resources to the reform efforts, it was important to delegate responsibilities and determine who would provide certain resources. When all of the resources were present and focused on the goals, the environment was resource rich, and all of the partners were able to focus on the goals. In turn, improved student learning was supported.

Appropriate Complexity

One of the most difficult aspects in a partnership of people from different backgrounds is developing the *appropriate complexity* pertaining to the project. The DESERT project demonstrates an appropriate level of complexity in terms of developing leadership capacity. In the beginning, a cadre of nine teachers was selected to become the DESERT staff. These collaborative teachers were given extensive professional development opportunities that included training in the process of change, evaluation tools, cognitive coaching techniques (Costa and Garmston 2002), science content, and science pedagogy. The collaborative teachers ultimately worked with school site science leaders and grade-based teacher leaders who were actively involved in studying their own instruction with the guidance of science education specialists.

During the professional development, teachers explored the instruction and culture in their schools with the assistance of the site science leader, and they participated in a professional development experience configured by the collaborative teacher. In this aspect of the program, teachers, district educators, scientists, and science educators were working side-by-side to create an environment that would ultimately support leadership capacity in the schools.

Practical and Soundly Constructed

Finally, partnerships need to be *practical* and *soundly constructed*. To have a functional partnership, all of the participants need to benefit from the partnership. In the DESERT project, teachers learned new ways to teach science, and they developed communities in which they could interact with one another and with local scientists and educators. In addition, they learned how to explore their own practice and determine the impact of their practice on student learning. The science educators explored teacher learning and developed new insights into school reform. The scientists learned how to create more interactive learning environments that allowed students to build their knowledge. At its simplest level, all of the participants benefited from the program, in that the practices espoused, enacted, or experienced were constantly discussed and demonstrated.

Principled Partnerships

"Take care of the sense, and the sounds will take care of themselves," [said the Duchess].

To foster change through partnerships, specific principles should be followed (see Figure 6.1, p. 70). These principles direct how the partners will interact with one another, the process by which the partners will achieve their goals, and the decisions made in the partnership. In the absence of guiding principles, the partnership's impact on student learning will be limited. These principles have strong parallels to the lessons learned in Chapter 5.

Figure 6.1

Principles for effective partnerships

* Involve important key members in the partnership in meaningful ways.
* Select a leader who facilitates the partnership rather than directs it.
* Build in ownership at all levels.
* Establish a communication and decision-making process that accepts disagreement, that allows for the resolution of conflict constructively, and that allows for decision making.
* Ensure that all members of the partnership know the goals and outcomes that result from the partnership.

Source: Adapted from Bell, J. A., and A. Buccino. 1997. *Seizing opportunities: Collaborating for excellence in teacher preparation.* Washington, DC: American Association for the Advancement of Science.

The first principle is a reminder that all key members should be *involved* or have opportunities to participate in the decisions made by the partnership. Teachers, as well as scientists, need to have countless opportunities to be involved in the partnership. By being involved in the discussions that form and facilitate the partnership, the concerns and ideas of all partners can be heard and addressed. Such involvement will help the team members understand their roles and responsibilities and will allow them to contribute to the intellectual component of the partnership.

In the DESERT project, teams of teachers, their administrators, school district science teachers, university scientists, and university science educators worked together to explore and support the use of inquiry in the science classroom. Administrators, scientists, and science educators discussed student learning, district expectations, and important concepts in science. Through these discussions, participants identified meaningful ways to be involved in the project. Meaningful participation was essential to program success, which leads to the second point.

The second principle concerns the *leadership* of a partnership. Selected leaders should be able to hear both sides of an argument and recognize valuable and insightful views, while simultaneously facilitating the growth of everyone involved. Good leaders have the ability to adjust and monitor the tensions between partners. Skills of negotiation and inclusion facilitate a partnership. A good leader also recognizes that partnerships evolve, resulting in different needs at different points in the partnership (see Chapter 5 for details). Expressing and resolving concerns involves identifying and clustering issues, defining relationships among them, and determining next steps to keep the partnership moving forward.

Good leadership is essential when partners are from different communities, such as universities and schools. Teachers and faculty members have different time demands and job expectations. These differences require both groups to understand how to work with one another. In developing the DESERT project, sound leadership was essential. The project director, who was responsible for developing the program and identifying the partners, was able to resolve tensions in the project as they emerged. For instance, after the initiation of site-based professional development, it became evident that different sites had different challenges. The director assisted in reaching project goals by providing differential support for each site, allowing for school-level autonomy. One result was expanded university offerings at the school site, allowing teachers to individualize their type of support.

Partnerships must also allow for *ownership*. Members should each be able to describe what contributions they make to the partnership. Not surprisingly, respect for the individual partners and ownership of project goals and processes are two sides of the same coin. By the end of the DESERT project, teachers and faculty members felt ownership in the project. The collaborative teachers, who were slated to return to the classroom, were anxious to find new avenues to support the professional development of their teachers. After five years of program support, inquiry learning activities in science were more evident, and teachers had increased both their pedagogical and content knowledge. As teachers left and new teachers were hired, the collaborative teachers convinced the district administrators to maintain their roles. Today, some are still serving in this capacity, while others work in university science teacher education programs.

As in any program that involves people, *communication* is paramount. Meeting times must be shared, decisions must be broadcast, and opportunities must exist to give and receive feedback. All information pertaining to the partnership needs to be accessible to the members, and all of the members should have the opportunity to interact with one another. With the increasing presence of technology, including web spaces and e-mail, communication can be fostered continually. Electronic archiving and messaging are only one aspect of communication. Communication also involves developing a shared language. Scientists, science educators, and teachers speak different languages. They must have time to develop a shared language and opportunities to build a common language. The ability to communicate within a partnership improves as opportunities are presented to meaningfully discuss aspects of the program.

In the DESERT project, communication existed at multiple levels. In the beginning, the director met with all potential collaborators to discuss the project. As the project began, communication was ongoing among teachers, administrators, and those involved in directing the project. Communication was essential in creating awareness and providing program information (see Levels of Use in Chapter 2). Once the project was up and going, there were monthly meetings with teachers, collaborative teachers, university faculty and staff, and administrators. Parents were notified periodically about the project to ensure they understood what their children were experiencing in science. As project funding decreased, meetings were held to ensure a degree of sustainability.

These conversations resulted in the university hiring a science liaison who would help coordinate science courses for local science teachers, as well as work with other districts to support their curriculum implementation. Generally speaking, the communication in this project was proactive and purposeful, and it resulted in structural changes that supported improved science teaching.

Finally, all members need to be *knowledgeable* about the parameters guiding the partnership. Knowledge of the goals and outcomes of the project will guide participation. In the DESERT project, a general statement about the goals of the project was constantly shared with all partners, including a timeline of suggested benchmarks for project accomplishments. This information enabled partners and participants to stay focused on project goals and reinforced expectations for participation.

Achieving a Partnership

"Who are YOU?" said the Caterpillar.
This was not an encouraging opening for a conversation. Alice replied, rather shyly, "I—I hardly know, sir, just at present—at least I know who I WAS when I got up this morning, but I think I must have been changed several times since then."

Partnerships are exciting and challenging when they start. There are new people with whom to talk and new resources available to access. Participants are excited to contribute and look forward to engaging in the planned events. Over time, the partners experience new learning and new avenues to collaboration. Although these outcomes have their own challenges, they represent program milestones. When the partnership impacts student learning, there is coherence and cause for celebration among participating members, allowing for optimism in the face of the inevitable problems that will occur.

This broad view of "commitment, new learning, and coherence" (Miles 1998, p. 55) characterizes the outside view of the partnership, which can be stable and consistent when principles have been put in place. Inside a partnership, however, partners may feel like Alice—rapidly changing and not always sure of their places. An external view of the partnership may be strong, but personal participation can reveal frustration and exhaustion (Bullough et al. 1999). Despite such personal feelings, partnerships can not only survive but can remain vibrant for many years if key partners remain dedicated to their goals and continually reflect on program progress. These results are true for the DESERT project. Although individuals may have questioned project success, a new relationship was forged between the university and school district that fostered inquiry teaching and science learning. The needs of individuals are important to recognize and acknowledge, but maintaining a view of the larger picture allows the partnership to accomplish its goals.

Good partnerships are not easy. They take time. They are built on good communication. They are based on clear goals. In science education, partnerships are critical in order to achieve the student learning outcomes outlined in the National Science Education Standards (NRC 1996). Teachers, administrators, scientists, and science educators (to name only a few) bring important experiences and knowledge to the reform of secondary science classrooms. Benefiting students will require the participation of all partners.

Going Forward

"Would you tell me, please, which way I ought to go from here?"
"That depends a good deal on where you want to get to," said the Cat.

When Alice landed in Wonderland, she had to negotiate her new environment. Here are some guiding questions as you begin *your* journey toward reform:

1. Who are the potential partners in your community interested in education? What skills and what goals might they bring to the partnership?
2. What are the goals of your project? How can all potential partners be involved in their development? How will you know if the goals are obtained?
3. How can good communication be fostered in the partnership?
4. How will the leadership of the partnership be fostered to support the project?
5. What are reasonable expectations for the project that involve all of the partners?

Recommended Resources

Sirotnik, K., and J. Goodlad, eds. 1988. *School-university partnerships in action: Concepts, cases, and concerns.* New York: Teachers College Press. The 12 essays in this book contemplate the design of school-university partnerships and provide examples from Goodlad's National Network for Educational Renewal.

Stephens, D., and G. Boldt. 2004. School/university partnerships: Rhetoric, reality, and intimacy. *Phi Delta Kappan* 85 (9): 703–707. This article explores partnership development and implications. Although this article focuses on preservice education, it is relevant to all aspects of science teacher education.

CONTEXTS OF SCIENCE EDUCATION REFORM

Using Data to Reform Science Instruction

Xiufeng Liu and Joseph Zawicki
State University of New York at Buffalo
Jeffrey Arnold
Daemen College

Frank, the Earth science teacher from across the hall, walked into Judy's room and asked, "Did you have a chance to analyze the results of the state exam?" Without waiting for a reply he continued, "Our students did a terrible job answering the questions related to wind and ocean currents once again this year. For example, only 50% of our students answered a question about the difference between air current, ocean current, and sea breeze correctly. The stronger students seemed to do just as poorly as the weaker students. I just don't understand it. These students have been exposed to the topic since middle school. We use videos and diagrams and hands-on labs on the causes of wind and ocean currents. I just don't know what more I can do."

Judy thought that the issue might be of interest to other teachers and suggested that they schedule an end-of-the-year science department meeting. At the meeting, Frank raised his concern about students consistently performing poorly on some topics. Some teachers found the issue to be interesting, as they had never examined students' performance by topics or questions. It hadn't occurred to them that test results could be used for improving instruction. A chemistry teacher suggested that Frank read an article about students' misconceptions and how students' misconceptions could be resistant to change unless they were explicitly challenged. The physics teacher commented that students seemed to be weak overall in interpreting graphs, as he assumed that questions related to wind and ocean currents involved complex graphs. Many other observations and suggestions were made. At the end of the meeting everyone felt the discussion had been useful because they had developed some specific ideas to try next year.

Frank read some of the research articles on student misconceptions and strategies to change them. Based on suggestions from research, he decided to teach the unit on wind and ocean currents differently from previous years. Before he started the unit, he spent one class period soliciting students' preconceptions and recording them on chart paper displayed in the front of the room. He also used online computer simulations to specifically address students' misconceptions about ocean currents.

Frank's efforts were rewarded. On the next state test, more than 80% of his students correctly answered questions related to the topic.

Frank's case illustrates several important benefits of examining student assessment data: Insight into student learning can be achieved, reading educational research can result in new ideas and instructional strategies, and student learning may be improved. This chapter will introduce you to skills and strategies used to examine classroom assessment data to improve science instruction. Although we advocate using multiple forms of student work to inform instruction, we will focus on using student responses to a statewide science assessment. Standardized tests, however, should by no means replace teacher-developed classroom assessments, particularly informal methods such as teacher observations and direct questioning. In general, the methods and techniques suggested in this chapter can be used to analyze any sample of scored student work.

From Data Giver to Data User

Why analyze student work or assessment data? One answer may be the prevalence of tests. The No Child Left Behind (NCLB) law has certainly accentuated the use of standardized assessments. Regardless of your opinion on increased testing, the goal of testing should be our primary focus: improving student achievement. The proactive use of assessment data can drive instructional changes and enable you to assume a leadership role in science education. Reforming science education is a systemic and collaborative effort. Leadership at the state, district, and school levels is important for initiating and sustaining reforms. Teacher leadership in the classroom, however, is a key to the success of all reforms. Student achievement will change little without changes in instruction.

Using assessment data to modify instruction reflects a role change from teacher as "data giver" to "data user." Typically, you act as a data giver when you report students' assessment results to the district, state, students, or parents. You act as a data user when you test hypotheses and conduct investigations using your own students' data to improve instruction. Assessment of students and effective instruction are fundamentally interconnected. By monitoring student learning on an ongoing basis, you can evaluate and adjust your teaching.

As stated in *National Science Education Standards*, "Far too often, more educational data are collected than analyzed or used to make decisions or take action" (NRC 1996, p. 90). Although controversy surrounds testing mandates, there is no controversy about the need to take full advantage of assessment data to make informed instructional decisions. Figure 7.1 presents four scenarios for testing and analysis. Increased standardized testing has moved all teachers toward more testing and data generation. You can choose between doing less analysis (quadrant IV) or more analysis (quadrant I).

"Using assessment data to modify instruction reflects a role change from teacher as 'data giver' to 'data user'."

Figure 7.1

Four scenarios involving testing and analysis

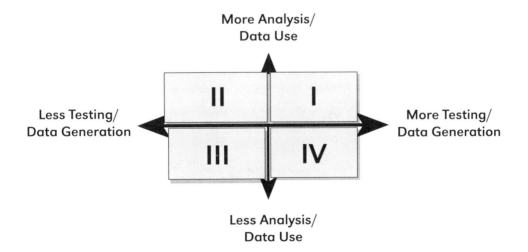

In choosing quadrant I, you move from data giver to data user, allowing you to identify areas for immediate instructional improvement, rather than having an instructional improvement plan imposed upon you. In the process, you are exerting professional leadership and contributing to the cause of science education reform.

Research has shown that inquiry into practice can be an effective tool to improve instruction, and assessment data can be a powerful source of knowledge and insight about teaching and student learning. As teachers, we often have specific student learning concerns. For example, in which areas are my students weak or strong? Which learning standards have my students mastered? Answering these questions requires you to go through an inquiry process. Similarly, in terms of instruction, you may have hunches about what works. Will spending more time on computers improve student learning? How is my teaching aligned with the state standards? Have I provided students sufficient opportunities to learn the material on which they will be tested? Obtaining clear answers to these questions requires you to gather and analyze data in order to test hypotheses prior to adjusting instructional practice.

Preparing for Data-Driven Instructional Improvement

Using data to improve instruction is a collective effort; an adequate infrastructure needs to be in place to support teachers. Establishing such an infrastructure includes examining beliefs, promoting collegiality, and gaining administrative support.

Teachers and school and district administrators must believe in the value of data-driven instructional improvement or such efforts will be only a slogan, at best. Using classroom data to improve instruction has an advantage. Unlike large-scale instructional improvements, which are often initiated by the school, district, or state, instructional improvement initiated by individual teachers usually involves one instructional aspect at a time—a more manageable rate of change. The effect of data-driven instructional improvement, however, may take some time to manifest tangible results. You must maintain confidence in the long-term benefit of using assessment to drive instructional change.

Using data to improve instruction is not the same as using test results to evaluate teachers. Using data helps establish a collegial atmosphere, allowing teachers to learn from each other. To be successful, teachers must feel secure in their professional roles. Such comfort empowers teachers to examine student performance critically and objectively as a reflection of the instructional program currently in place, not as a personal deficiency. A collaborative and ongoing review of data is essential to maintaining a vibrant school instructional program. (Chapter 5 suggests strategies for building and sustaining group collaboration and leadership within your school.)

To benefit from the analysis of assessment data, school and district administrators need to provide support in terms of teacher time, professional development opportunities, resources, and incentives. For example, assistance in entering student test responses can be a tremendous source of support. This process can be accomplished with optical scanning devices (e.g., a Scantron) that can be saved in the form of a text file or by contracting professionals to conduct data analysis. Both these processes can save you valuable time and speed up the data analysis process. Regardless of analysis technique, you will still need to be supported in interpreting analysis results and developing instructional improvement plans.

Conducting Data Analysis

Various data analysis tools are available, some of them free. Because using data to improve instruction primarily involves descriptive and simple inferential statistical analysis, general purpose computer packages such as Microsoft Office Excel are sufficient. The advantage of using a spreadsheet program such as Excel is its availability at school and home and on any computer platform (PC or Mac computers). You may also be able to locate automatic or semiautomatic data analysis templates that are either computer-based Excel worksheets or internet-based Java applets. One sample data analysis template that can perform all the data analyses discussed in this chapter is available at *www.buffalo.edu/~xliu5/template.xls*. This template contains a number of Excel worksheets. Once students' responses are entered, common statistical analysis results are produced automatically.

Data analysis typically involves the following steps: entering and scoring student responses, conducting item analysis, conducting test analysis, interpreting data analysis results, and planning for instructional improvement.

Entering and Scoring Student Responses

Whatever computer programs or tools you may choose, the first step in data analysis is entering student responses into a data table. Table 7.1 is an example that may be used for this purpose. Note the key information that is included. Although the designation of rows and columns as either "student" or "item" fields is arbitrary, the table must include a scoring key to multiple-choice questions and the possible credit assigned to multiple-choice or constructed-response questions. Multiple-choice questions are usually assigned 1 credit for a correct response and 0 credits for an incorrect response. In many cases, the program you are using can do this task for you. For constructed-response questions, the number of credits students earned (e.g., 0, 1, 2, 3, etc.) should be entered into the table. A student's total score and percentage score (the total score divided by total number of points) is easily calculated from the table. Once students' responses are scored, statistical analyses can be performed on individual items (item analysis), groups of items, or the entire test (test analysis).

Table 7.1

A sample format for entering student responses

Item	Keys/Points	Student 1	Student 2	Student 3	Student 4
Q1	A	A	A	A	A
Q2	A	A	B	A	D
Q3	D	D	A	A	D
			....		
CR25	1	1	1	1	0
CR26	1	1	0	1	0
CR27	2	1	1	2	1
			....		

Note: Q = multiple choice, CR = constructed response.

Conducting Item Analysis

Now that you have input and scored student responses, you are ready to analyze student performance by test item.

Analyzing item difficulty. Item difficulty refers to the percent or proportion of students who have answered a question correctly for multiple-choice questions or percent or proportion of credits students earned out of the total possible credits for constructed-response questions. If 159 students answer a multiple-choice test question, and 154 students answer the item correctly, then the item difficulty is 97% or 0.97 (Q1 in Table 7.2). In this example, the percentage of students responding incorrectly would be 3% or 0.03. Similarly, if on average students earned only 1.5 credits out of 2.0 for a constructed-response question, then the item difficulty is 75% or 0.75 (CR27 in Table 7.2). Items are not particularly useful for instructional improvement when all or almost all of your students answer the item correctly or incorrectly.

Table 7.2

Sample item difficulties and discriminations

Item	Difficulty	Discrimination
Q1	0.97	0.18
Q2	0.50	0.60
Q3	0.41	-0.05
	....	
CR25	0.55	0.42
CR26	0.27	0.67
CR27	0.75	0.13
	....	

The most intriguing (and useful) items are often those with difficulties between 0.30 and 0.80 because they tend to differentiate students by those who have mastered the material and those who have not.

Analyzing item discrimination. Item discrimination is the correlation between students' performance on a particular item with their overall performance on the test. Computer tools such as Excel can perform this analysis. Correlations of less than 0.30 suggest that the test question may be flawed—confusing, too difficult or too easy, or miskeyed—or the concept may not have been taught correctly (e.g., Q1 in Table 7.2). Negative correlation is the worst scenario; it indicates that more able students tend to answer the question incorrectly and less able students tend to answer the question correctly.

Analyzing response pattern. The response pattern for an item indicates the number of students selecting each of the alternative responses for multiple-choice items or the number of students receiving no, partial, or full credit for constructed-response items. Response patterns can indicate the degree to which students have a good understanding of a concept or the number of students with common misconceptions.

Figures 7.2 and 7.3 show two items from the 2003 New York State eighth-grade science exam *(see www.nysedregents.org/testing/sciei/sciences8.html)*. Item analysis results from the two sample questions are listed in Table 7.3, page 84.

Figure 7.2

Sample question 1 (Q1) shows two dogs pulling on a rope with constant but unequal forces.

In which compass direction will both dogs most likely move?
A. east
B. west
C. north
D. south

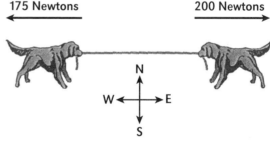

175 Newtons   200 Newtons

Source: 2003 New York State eighth-grade science exam, *www.nysedregents.org/testing/sciei/sciences8.html.*

Figure 7.3

Sample question 2 (Q2) involves ocean currents and air mass.

Which factor has the greatest influence on the direction of the air-mass track?
A. Upper air current
B. Ocean currents
C. Sea breezes
D. Mountain barriers

Source: 2003 New York State eighth-grade science exam, *www. nysedregents.org/testing/sciei/sciences8.html.*

Table 7.3

Sample item response pattern

Item	Key	Difficulty	Discrimination	A	B	C	D
Q1	A	0.97	0.18	154 (96.9%)	3 (1.9%)	1 (0.6%)	1 (0.6%)
Q2	A	0.50	0.60	79 (49.6%)	26 (16.4%)	27 (17.0%)	27 (17.0%)

The discrimination coefficient for item Q1 is 0.18. This low discrimination is attributable to the low difficulty score of 0.97, meaning that 97% (154 out of 159) of the students answered the item correctly by choosing A; almost no students selected other choices. The high success rate suggests that students have learned the topic very well or that the question is easy and it does not differentiate students who have a good understanding from those who do not. As a result, the question is not particularly useful in guiding instructional improvement.

The difficulty index for Q2 is 0.50. For this question, half of the students selected incorrect answers. The discrimination coefficient is 0.60, a modestly high correlation, suggesting that more able students answered the question correctly more often than less able students. Approximately half of the students answered the question correctly, with an approximately equal number selecting incorrect choices. The response pattern may indicate that, though a large number of students had a good understanding of the concept related to Q2, choices B, C, and D could represent common misconceptions among many students. If the majority of the students selected a single incorrect response, the pattern may indicate a misconception or a mistake in the answer key. Both issues are important to explore.

Conducting Test Analysis

In addition to examining student performance on individual test items, you can also use computer programs such as Excel to examine student performance on groups of questions related to various learning standards, review the achievement of different groups of students (class 1 versus class 2, boys versus girls, etc.), or examine how your instruction is aligned with the curriculum standard and the test. This type of analysis involves classification of items into various groups and calculation of average item difficulty over all items within each group.

Analyzing mastery of standards. By grouping items based on curriculum standards and calculating the average of item difficulties, you can determine the percentage of the standard students have mastered. The higher the percentage, the better the mastery level students have achieved. For example, Table 7.4 shows that there are five items related to Standard 1 (S1), and the average difficulty for the five items is .5, meaning that students have mastered 50% of S1.

Table 7.4

Sample results on student mastery of standards

Standard	S1	S2	S3	...
No. of Items	5	8	6	
Average Difficulty	0.5	0.8	0.3	

A similar analysis may also be conducted by using different cognitive levels, such as those defined in Bloom's taxonomy. Questions at a particular cognitive level are grouped together, and the average of difficulties of those questions is calculated as an indication of students' performance on the cognitive level. For example, it may be useful to find out if students have done well on items requiring application and analysis, as opposed to simple recall.

Analyzing alignment. The alignment among curriculum, instruction, and assessment is essential to ensure high levels of student learning. One simple way to analyze the alignment is to represent curriculum, instruction, and assessment in three columns of a table. A check mark (✓) is placed in the cell if a standard has been taught during instruction and if it is present in the test. Table 7.5 is a sample alignment table.

Table 7.5

Sample alignment table

Learning Standards	Well Taught?	Present in Test?
1a. Living things are composed of cells. Cells provide structure and carry on major functions to sustain life. Cells are usually microscopic in size.	✓	✓
1b. The way in which cells function is similar in all living things. Cells grow and divide, producing more cells. Cells take in nutrients, which they use to provide energy for the work that cells do and to make the materials that a cell or an organism needs.	✓	
1c. Most cells have cell membranes, genetic material, and cytoplasm. Some cells have a cell wall and/or chloroplasts. Many cells have a nucleus.		✓
1d. Some organisms are single cells; others, including humans, are multicellular.		

In the example in Table 7.5, Learning Standards 1a and 1b were both taught, but only Standard 1a was addressed on the test. A gap in instruction existed for Standards 1c and 1d, because neither standard was well taught, although only 1c was on the test. A simple percentage of checked standards out of the total number of standards for the second and third columns can be calculated as a measure of alignment between instruction and curriculum standards (e.g., 50%) and between the test coverage and curriculum standards (e.g., 45%). As for the alignment between instruction and test coverage, a percentage of standards checked in both columns out of the total number of standards can be calculated as a measure for alignment (e.g., 70%). Alternatively, a correlation between instructional coverage and test coverage of the learning standards may be calculated by assigning a value of 1 to each cell with a check mark and 0 to each cell without (e.g., 56%).

Conducting other analyses. Depending on your interests for instructional improvement, you may want to explore questions that require you to input new data. The methods to be used are similar to those previously described. For example, you may wish to analyze student performances based on question format (multiple choice, constructed response, and performance assessment), learning topic, class period, or preparation in mathematics or reading. Student group performance differences, based on gender or race, for example, may also be analyzed. For example, if you know that there is an achievement gap among students of different cultures, and you have been implementing strategies such as those suggested in Chapter 8, you can conduct data analysis to find out if the achievement gap has indeed been narrowed.

Interpreting Data Analysis Results and Planning for Instructional Improvement

Data analysis is only the beginning of the data-driven instructional improvement process. Once these data are available, teachers must take the time to make sense of it. To interpret data analysis results and identify areas for instructional improvement, teachers need to keep an open mind. Many factors impact student understanding and performance, such as the quality of test items, teacher instruction, and student learning. A Data Analysis Results Interpretation Sheet, such as the one shown in Table 7.6, can help tell the story behind the results.

Table 7.6

Data analysis results interpretation sheet

Category	Student Performance	Student Factors	Test Factors	Instructional Factors
Q1	Difficulty: 0.97 Discrimination: 0.18	None	Item flaw	None
Q2	Difficulty: 0.50 Discrimination: 0.60	Misconception Unable to differentiate concepts	Diagram difficult to read	Not enough time spent on differentiating concepts
Standard S1	Difficulty: 0.5	Topic too abstract	None	Instruction rushed; need more hands-on

In Table 7.6, the first column is the category of analysis, which can be individual test questions, standards, cognitive levels, student subgroups, etc. The second column shows the results of the data analysis indicating students' performances, such as difficulty and discrimination. The other three columns are possible reasons contributing to the performance levels in column 2. Student factors include considerations such as students' content knowledge, the reading level or readability of a particular question, misconceptions, the amount of effort the student brings to the assessment, student reasoning patterns, and so on. Testing factors may include item difficulty and discrimination, item placement in the test (Is a difficult item placed too close to the beginning of a test?), distracting or confusing graphics, unique item style, or a poorly written question.

In addition, teachers may have not taught the concept, may have taught the topic too briefly, or may have taught the idea inadequately. Sincere self-reflection and a frank discussion with colleagues is needed to elicit all potential causes. A careful analysis of this sort will indicate concepts that should be addressed during the program review. Once causes for students' poor performances have been identified, you can follow up with specific actions and develop instructional improvement plans.

Data analysis can also be used to improve the quality of test questions. For instance, Table 7.6 shows that the difficulty for Q1 was 0.97. The discrimination for the item was 0.18. As described earlier, 154 students selected the correct answer A, three selected response B, and only one student selected responses C and D. This item was among the easiest on the test. The vast majority of students were able to answer this question correctly. Notice that the item does not assess a student's ability to relate mass to force or to other, perhaps more challenging, concepts. Choices C and D could be eliminated by test-wise students immediately without much conceptual understanding, leaving only choices A and B as plausible responses. Thus, student success could be attributed to a flaw in the item itself, not necessarily to students' understanding. As a result of this analysis, Q1 should be rewritten or replaced.

The data in Table 7.6 suggests that student performance on Q2 was not satisfactory. Earlier data indicated that 79 students selected the correct answer A, 26 selected response B, 27 selected response C, and 27 selected response D. Only half of the students in this sample recognized the role of upper air currents in moving the tropical air mass from the Gulf of Mexico to the northeastern United States. The discrimination value for this item was moderately high (0.60), indicating that, although more able students tend to have answered the question correctly, some more able students may have been confused, as well. The majority of the students answering this question incorrectly indicated the role of either ocean currents or sea breezes.

Overall, the response pattern for this question is clearly not random—students selected choices B, C, and D almost evenly. In this case, the teacher explained the three concepts (i.e., air current, ocean current, and sea breeze) during classroom instruction, but expected students to differentiate these ideas on their own. The data support the conclusion that a misconception may exist in which students believe that air currents, ocean currents, and sea breezes are the same thing. Accordingly, one instructional improvement may involve computer simulations requiring students to differentiate among the three concepts. Chapter 2 provides a synthesis of current research on how students learn and may give you additional ideas about how you may initiate and sustain instructional improvements.

Going Further

Using data to improve instruction is an open-ended process. Depending on the availability of resources and time, you can start with small-scale, focused instructional improvement and gradually expand the efforts to cover more areas of instruction. More powerful instructional improvements may be the ones coordinated among teachers or those that become part of the entire school or district instructional improvement plans. Various resources are available to take teachers further. These resources can be found in the Recommended Resources section that follows.

Recommended Resources

Bernhardt, V. L. 1998. *Data analysis for comprehensive school-wide improvement.* Larchmont, NY: Eye Education. This book offers an easy-to-follow, step-by-step guide to conduct data analysis for comprehensive schoolwide improvement.

Diagnoser.com *(www.diagnoser.com/diagnoser/index.jsp).* Funded by the National Science Foundation, this comprehensive website contains a large collection of diagnostic assessment questions related to major concepts in high school physics. Teachers can use a subset of questions to solicit students' misconceptions and select classroom-tested activities to help students change their incorrect misconceptions.

Holcomb, E. L. 1999. *Getting excited about data: How to combine people, passion, and proof.* **Thousand Oaks, CA: Corwin Press**. This book provides a useful conceptual framework and techniques on how data may be used to improve teaching and learning at the school level.

Love, N. 2002. *Using data/getting results: A practical guide for school improvement in mathematics and science.* **Norwood, MA: Christopher-Gordon Publishers.** This book provides useful conceptual frameworks and techniques on how data may be used to improve teaching and learning at the school level.

Popham, J. W. 1990. *Modern educational measurement: A practitioner's perspective.* **Englewood Cliffs, NJ: Prentice Hall.** This easy-to-read, highly practical book provides the background to all the measurement and statistics topics discussed in this chapter.

Appropriate Practice for Linguistically Diverse Science Learners

Carla C. Johnson
University of Cincinnati

Maria, a seventh-grade student in an urban middle school in the Southwest, has lived in the United States with her family off and on for five years. Maria's father works as a laborer on a farm. Her mother is a housekeeper and works part-time at a grocery store in the evenings. She has two younger siblings: a sister in fourth grade and a four-year-old brother. Maria's family goes back to Mexico three or four times each year. These trips have an impact on her school performance. She spends most of her time just trying to keep up. Maria finds it difficult to follow along even when she is in school. With her frequent border crossings, her Spanish was never fully developed and provides a poor basis on which to learn English. Although she understands basic conversational English, she struggles with reading and comprehension.

Maria's teacher, Mr. Morris, believes Maria "just doesn't get it" most of the time, along with the other 15 Mexican students in his fourth-hour class of 28 students. He says, "The Mexican students in my class are just slower than the others. I teach and the other kids in the class understand, but the Mexican students can't tell me anything about what we have learned after we do an experiment. It is like it just goes over their heads." Maria's limited vocabulary inhibits her ability to verbalize what she has learned or record her thoughts in science journals. Mr. Morris also has limited awareness of his students' background knowledge and experiences. Though he tries to provide concrete examples of science concepts in class, students like Maria have limited experience with amusement parks and Jell-O.

Maria's low confidence in her ability to do science is due, in part, to the low expectations Mr. Morris has for her. Maria, however, enjoys learning about science and is making slow progress, but her learning could be accelerated if she was taught in a culturally relevant way. This chapter will outline suggestions for science teachers to consider in making their science teaching more effective for English language learners.

Need for Culturally Relevant Science

The population of the United States continues to become increasingly diverse, both culturally and linguistically. In less than two decades, one half of the students in the United States will be non-white and Latino, with one quarter of the total student body speaking a language other than English (Garcia 2002). Presently in the United States, at least 17% of the 5- to 24-year-old population speaks a native language other than English, and at least 8% of students receive English language services in school (NCES 2003).

English language learners also perform significantly behind their native-English-speaking peers in science, as shown in the 2000 National Assessment of Educational Progress, on which Latinos scored 20 points lower than white students. In addition, nearly 40% of middle school Latino students are performing below grade level in all subjects and experience high school drop-out rates two to three times that of white students (Garcia 2002). These differences constitute a crisis for language minority students in U.S. schools that will require an instructional shift if the achievement gap in science is to narrow.

Fortunately, science has a great potential to bridge cultural and linguistic gaps. Science topics are interesting and provide a concrete mechanism for engaging students while they develop literacy skills, that is, skills in reading, writing, listening, and speaking. Two types of language are important for students to use in science: social and academic. Social language is interpersonal and dependent on culture, including tone of voice, facial expressions, and body language. Academic language is more complex and cognitively demanding and is the language most commonly used in school. In science classrooms, both forms of language can be easily employed. The result is a science classroom that can improve students' understanding of science, assist in the development of their academic literacy skills, and demonstrate the important role science plays in their daily lives as well as in future careers.

Unfortunately, many teachers have limited preparation in teaching a second language in the context of subject matter. Traditional science instruction in the United States typically places white, English-speaking students at an advantage, as it relies heavily on teacher-centered delivery of content knowledge through lecture and provides little opportunity for student involvement and exploration. As a result, non-white students do not see cultural, language, or interactional connections with the subject being taught and are educationally disadvantaged (Gibbons 2003). To better meet the needs of English language learners, science teachers must learn to use student-centered strategies, such as cooperative learning and inquiry, to make science meaningful and comprehensible to all students. This chapter focuses on strategies you can use to enable *all* students to be successful while embracing the added diversity in your classroom.

Research-Based Strategies for Culturally Responsive Teaching

The instructional congruence framework (Lee and Fradd 2001) has been developed to guide teachers in making their science instruction more culturally relevant. It includes purposeful attention to science content knowledge, inquiry, language, and cultural experience. Instructional congruence includes four components: students, teachers, science, and literacy. These components will act as the organizers for the rest of this chapter. Through the use of the instructional congruence framework, you can enable students to increase their learning of science as they increase literacy and English language skills, making academic content and inquiry accessible, meaningful, and relevant for diverse students.

Students

In order to support student learning, you must get to know students individually. While doing so, you will discover both their needs and the value of a diverse student body in the science classroom. For instance, English language learners often have a different set of experiences that can help the class attain a broader understanding of science. When discussing concepts such as seasons, weather, or animals, linguistic minority students may bring unique background knowledge or experience. This information can be invaluable in helping you adjust your instruction. When learning about your linguistic minority students, consider issues related to language barriers, differences in cultural norms, and areas of student interest.

Language Barriers. Linguistic minority students are often years behind their peers in both literacy and language development, including the areas of reading, writing, listening, and speaking. Even though students may have functional social language skills, academic language may be much less complete and often takes five to seven years to develop. To help, you must emphasize science vocabulary and concept development. To increase student confidence with the academic language of science, consider having your students use their home language in class for communication or for building new vocabulary in English. Students may illustrate the content they are learning by linking the pictures to the academic vocabulary. Consistent reinforcement in this area will increase the speed at which students are able to articulate what they have learned in class.

Cultural Norms. Cultures vary from place to place. A cultural norm describes the ways people interact with one another and their environments. Even within the United States, cultures and norms vary. Just think about the differences in interactional styles of individuals from Kentucky, New York City, or North Dakota! One norm that varies across culture has to do with authority. Respecting authority, particularly elders, is a centerpiece of many cultures. In some cultures, questioning an adult or an idea offered by an adult is considered inappropriate and disrespectful. When learning science, however, we want students to question ideas, each other, and the concepts presented by teachers. Students often have difficulty with this type of learning environment until they have had many experiences in this setting.

To assist in this process, establish clear classroom expectations. Provide examples of appropriate student-to-student and student-to-teacher interactions. A discussion web is one way to do this. In this process, students are asked to answer a question with a yes or no answer and then discuss it with a partner. For instance, "Plants grow because of the food they get from the dirt" could open up a lively discussion, allowing students to explore background knowledge and preconceptions in a nonthreatening way. Following this conversation, you can introduce a reading or a demonstration or can conduct an activity that allows students to further explore this idea, allowing students to reconsider the validity of their original choice. This process helps students use academic language while questioning statements by the teacher, other students, or written materials.

To learn more about your students, their interests, their families, and their cultural norms, consider accessing cultural advisers, conducting home visits, and, ultimately, connecting science to student cultures. *Cultural advisers* can be parents, school aides, or community members who can help you navigate the cultural terrain and learn more about your students and their backgrounds. Cultural advisers are also great sources of wisdom about how to address potential student or parent concerns. These advisers can share with you acceptable and unacceptable practices that can have an impact on your relationships with students and their families. For instance, a cultural adviser will know if visiting a student's home is appropriate if the husband is not there or if offering a small token of your appreciation is acceptable or expected following a visit. Cultural advisers may also be able to recommend community members who might act as guest speakers, enabling students to see individuals from diverse cultures engaged in science-related careers.

After getting to know your students in the classroom context, consider conducting home visits. Target students whom you find interesting or puzzling or whose parents are willing to invite you for a visit. Prior to the visit, explain to the family that you are there to learn about their child's interests so that you can more effectively teach science. Make an appointment at a time when the student, father, and mother (as appropriate) can be present. In Latino cultures, it may be seen as inappropriate to visit the home without the father present. Keep the visit short, but come prepared with a few specific questions. Questions could include, "What kinds of activities do you participate in as a family?" or "What hobbies do you enjoy?" While you are in the home, make note of books, family activities, toys, or other elements that you could tie into your science instruction.

Student Interest. Connecting a student's experiences to school science is an important step in making science relevant. One way to do this is to create a science-at-home project. In this project, students can take or draw pictures of examples of science such as cooking, cleaning, or gardening. Using the illustration, the students can explain verbally or in writing the reason they picked the example and how it relates to school science. Through classroom presentations, all students and the teacher can learn more about connections between everyday life and science.

Areas of student interest can provide an engaging place to start your science instruction. At the beginning of the year, have students brainstorm a list of topics, interests, and experiences that go along with your curriculum. Ways to capitalize on these interests may include a science fair or in-class science projects. Several websites exist that have science interest surveys. Completing such surveys will help your students narrow their interests. As a result of these projects, consider creating a science night, inviting parents and their students to visit the school.

Finally, situate your science learning in the context of the real world, demonstrating how science impacts our everyday lives. Use current events such as space technology, bird flu, hurricanes, or the changing seasons. Whenever possible, link current events to the students' background knowledge, experiences, or interests. For example, exploring the science of cooking may be an interesting way to explore chemistry. Examining foods, spices, and medicinal herbs from around the world may act as an introduction to botany and use of plants.

Teachers

We continue to learn more and more about the factors that impact learning in the science classroom. Not surprising, individual teacher effectiveness is the greatest predictor of student success (Johnson, Kahle, and Fargo 2007). Consider the following vignette from the classroom of an effective teacher, Ms. Miller.

Students are comfortable learning in Ms. Miller's science class. Class always starts in a similar way, with a question on the white board. Today's question is, "What does this (↓) have to do with what we have been learning in science so far this year?"

"Individual teacher effectiveness is the greatest predictor of student success."

An arrow points from the board to a tortilla press, which Ms. Miller demonstrates. The students consult their pre-assigned partners, discuss the question aloud, and then respond in writing in their science journals. After a few minutes, one student answers, "We think it is chemical and physical changes—as the flour and water are mixed and become dough." Another student answers, "Isn't that a machine, a simple machine, the press?" Others make additional connections.

Thanking the students for their ideas, Ms. Miller indicates that all the answers were well thought out and that simple machines will be the topic explored in class today. On the board she writes "Simple Machines," followed by words and pictures of common simple machines. Posters of levers, screws, inclined planes, and wedges cover the board. As a review, Ms. Miller pulls objects out of a box one by one and asks students to identify the simple machine the object represents. Ms. Miller assigns each item to a small group to construct a picture, record the name of the simple machine represented, and then place it on the word wall (a systematic collection of words displayed in large letters to provide vocabulary reference and support during reading and writing).

Following this activity, students gather into their preassigned cooperative learning teams where they receive their "challenge" from Ms. Miller: a letter from Really Good Food Company asking them to create a simple machine that could be used to make a new kind of snack food. Objectives listed on the board include the development of a time line for completing a blueprint design, a model, and an infomercial, in which students will make a presentation to sell their product. Students are each assigned a role—architect, recorder, engineer, or builder. Each student group is then given a box of items they can use to build their machines.

As teams engage in early brainstorming, Ms. Miller circulates among the groups providing guidance, praise, and clarification—but not the answer. She observes how the work in each team is unfolding. To support this work, she asks questions that help her understand her students' thinking as they practice expressing ideas related to the simple machine vocabulary illustrated and listed on the board.

In this example, Ms. Miller has used many of the right strategies to support her students. First, she has created *a structured learning environment* where students know the routines that allow the class to flow smoothly. Elements such as starting the class with work on the board, or knowing how and where to collect and return materials, make science learning a comfortable place in which to take cognitive and linguistic risks.

Second, Ms. Miller has set *high expectations*. She believes that all students in her class are capable of learning and she communicates that expectation to students on a regular basis. Students are accountable for starting class on time, expected to engage in meaningful conversations with partners, and assigned a role on a team with the responsibility to produce a product.

Third, Ms. Miller has provided her students with *challenging work* in which they are being asked to solve problems by thinking like scientists. The content, simple machines, comes from the state science standards. Her presentation allowed all students to start from a *common experience*, the use of a tortilla press, and translate this experience and prior knowledge to a novel situation, the creation of a machine to make a new snack. The lesson itself combines *multiple opportunities for students to practice using social and academic language* in multiple formats: small-group brainstorming, recording ideas, drawing blueprints, building models, and designing an infomercial. These multiple modes of interaction accelerate both content knowledge and literacy skill development in English language learners. In fact, research has shown that these methods are more effective than reading terminology-laden textbooks.

Finally, Ms. Miller *continually assessed student learning* by interacting with student teams, asking questions of individuals, and observing student interaction. Through pointed questions, Ms. Miller could determine if conceptual understanding was taking place or she could address potential misconceptions. By focusing on the individual student, Ms. Miller could modify lessons to ensure that all students succeed. Depending on student needs, success-minded modifications may include practicing vocabulary, working with reading comprehension, recording ideas in words or in pictures, and pairing a student to work with a peer.

Science

The instructional congruence framework considers science broadly as defined in the National Science Education Standards (NSES) (NRC 1996). The major subcategories within science include the following:

1. Learning key science concepts as well as big ideas in terms of patterns of change, systems, models, and relationships (knowing)
2. Conducting science inquiry emphasizing students' asking questions and finding answers (doing)
3. Engaging in science discourse and multiple representations using various written and oral communication formats (talking)
4. Having scientific habits of mind in terms of the values, attitudes, and world views in science (thinking)

In the following section, these ideas will be used to describe important elements of science teaching while a classroom example weaves the ideas together.

Science Standards, Science Concepts, and Big Ideas (Knowing). When planning for culturally relevant science teaching, start with the national and state science standards. By targeting the science concepts students should learn, you can streamline your instruction while expanding opportunities to reinforce language and literacy development.

A critical component of learning for all students is to help them connect ideas. For instance, the rock cycle is a common topic in middle-level science. As described in the NSES, the big idea surrounding the rock cycle is as follows:

> *Some changes in the solid earth can be described as the "rock cycle." Old rocks at the earth's surface weather, forming sediments that are buried, then compacted, heated, and often crystallized into new rock. Eventually, those new rocks may be brought to the surface by the forces that drive plate motions, and the rock cycle continues.* (Grades 5–8, Content Standard D, p. 160)

In essence, the rock cycle is about breaking down Earth's materials and building them back up. How can this idea be used to help students organize their thinking in a culturally relevant way? Consider posting pictures of different types of landscapes: mountains, rock faces, deserts, beaches, glaciers, streambeds, etc. Give each picture a label using the rock cycle associated vocabulary (*weathering, erosion, sedimentation*) to reinforce the associated vocabulary. Then ask students in pairs or small teams to describe how one landscape may change to look like another. This activity will allow students to hypothesize processes that occur in nature, particularly weathering, while using social and academic language. The idea of a cycle can be introduced, both verbally and pictorially, to act as an organizer for the content in the rest of the unit.

Inquiry and Student-Centered Science Instruction (Doing). Inquiry learning provides students with the opportunity to explore a question, bringing to bear prior knowledge. If your students have not had much experience with student-centered instruction, you may need to provide more guidance and multiple opportunities for student practice. Many inquiry-based lessons have students working in small groups with a question or problem to solve.

Rock classification activities are good places to start using inquiry. Instead of the typical prescribed rock identification lab, you can pose an inquiry twist by giving students a box of unknown rocks and asking them to develop a classification system that they will present to the class. This activity focuses student attention on the characteristics of the rocks while providing multiple correct answers, such as size, color, grain size, or scratch tests. Beyond small-group observation and exploration, you may provide supplemental resources, such as access to the internet, rock identification booklets, or materials to perform rock identification tests.

Engaging in Science Discourse (Talking). Cooperative learning groups facilitate science learning while promoting discourse between the teacher and students, among students in groups, and across groups. Successful cooperative grouping techniques not only place students in groups, but include the assignment of student roles. This process facilitates task completion and holds students individually and collectively accountable.

For English language learners, it is important to have multiple ways to present their science thinking and learning. Written products include word walls, science journals, and stories. Oral products include small-group work, such as think-pair-share or jigsaw groups, or class presentations that may include stories and songs. Pictorial products may involve illustrated vocabulary cards or posters, charts, or tables to share findings. Word walls are particularly effective because they can act as a reference during class, providing practice and reinforcement for new vocabulary.

To complete the rock inquiry, have each group construct a poster on which the group organizes its data and presents its categorization scheme. As the small groups negotiate the observation and classification process, they develop communication skills, justify decisions, and participate in multiple modes of data presentation. Learning may take place in a nonthreatening, feedback-rich setting that requires the use of science vocabulary and context-relevant speech. The opportunities to discuss and practice using the new vocabulary further provide students with the ability to understand concepts in class while improving their English literacy.

Scientific Habits of Mind (Thinking). Scientific habits of mind include the values, attitudes, and skills used in science and problem solving. Habits of mind include the use of effective communication, appropriate use of quantitative measurements, and critical thinking. These habits of mind are not only important in science classrooms, but are transferable to real-world contexts and are a key characteristic of a scientifically literate individual. The only way to develop these skills is through experience in conducting real science.

In the rock inquiry, you provide students with a problem to solve. Instead of reading about science and answering recall questions, students engage in doing science—thinking like scientists to determine what to test, how to classify, and how to display their findings. Through these learning experiences, deep conceptual understanding takes place while students engage in scientific thought and discourse. Through concrete experiences, students learn that there are multiple correct answers in science from which to choose, based on the quality of the explanations and evidence provided. You can ask students to make observations, organize and present information, form conclusions, and justify their outcomes while evaluating the work of others.

Literacy

Literacy development includes skills in reading, writing, and other forms of communication in formal and informal settings. This chapter concludes with three general strategies that can be used to help increase literacy development.

Writing in Science. Writing should be a daily component of all secondary science classrooms, whether through a daily question on the board, daily student science journals, personal narratives (storytelling), learning new vocabulary words and definitions, or writing a laboratory procedure. Linguistic minority students who are working on improving their English literacy will benefit from multiple opportunities to write about science. For instance, a student could create a personal word wall where he or she writes, defines, and illustrates science words in his or her journal. This process provides practice as well as creates a reference for science terminology. Lab reports can ask students to use narrative writing to describe their questions, hypotheses, procedures, analyses, and conclusions. Prewriting and outlines can be used with all classroom-based assignments as a means for teachers to assess progress and for peers to provide feedback.

Reading in Science. Reading traditional textbooks can present a formidable challenge to English language learners. To accommodate all readers in your classroom, include reading activities with pictures and readings targeted to varying reading levels. Scaffold reading proficiency by pairing students with a reading partner. This strategy uses fewer books and offers students an opportunity to see, hear, and speak to each other as they read. Many supplemental reading materials now exist that offer leveled readers (small, concept-targeted books) and diagnostic tools for the teacher to determine appropriate reading levels. Supplemental readers, such as ConceptLinks by Millmark Education, offer a series developed specifically for English language learners. Finally, audiobooks can help students build literacy through listening and reading along with the text.

Visual Representations. Visual representations of concepts can be found through internet simulations, detailed color photographs, diagrams, charts, tables, and manipulatives. Various visuals can supplement the textbook and help students identify key concepts prior to or concurrent with reading. Visuals are especially important when teaching abstract concepts that are not easily supported by hands-on materials. For instance, a number of online resources related to cell structure provide high-quality images that can be shown to the class through an LCD projector and computer. There are several physics-related sites that offer roller coaster simulations with which students can build their own coaster and test out the design. The Ohio Resource Center for Mathematics, Science, and Reading has prescreened links to sites that it considers effective for students (see *www.ohiorc.org*). And don't forget to use graphs or tables to illustrate relationships in ways that may be more accessible to all students.

Maria in a Different Light

Maria, the student who was discussed at the opening of this chapter, is now in the 10th grade. Her teacher, Mrs. Jennings, completed a summer professional development program designed to make her science instruction more effective for linguistic minorities. Each day, Maria and her classmates engage in science directly tied to the real world. One day she told Mrs. Jennings, "I believe all students can learn science. The key to enabling them to learn is to have them express themselves and relate what they are learning in school to their lives and their background." As a result, Maria has increased her English literacy, is more interested in learning science, and feels more capable of success. In fact, Maria told Mrs. Jennings that she likes science and is considering becoming a medical assistant or a veterinarian when she graduates from high school.

Recommended Resources

Fathman, A. K., and D. T. Crowther. 2006. *Science for English language learners: K–12 classroom strategies*. Arlington, VA: NSTA Press. A wealth of specific English language learner instructional activities for K–12 science; a must-have resource for teachers of diverse learners.

Garcia, E. 2002. *Student cultural diversity: Understanding and meeting the challenge*. 3rd ed. Boston: Houghton Mifflin. Describes in detail the characteristics of culturally diverse students, their associated strengths, and their challenges to learning.

Hill, J. D., and K. M. Flynn. 2006. *Classroom instruction that works with English language learners*. Alexandria, VA: Association for Supervision and Curriculum Development. Research-based strategies that have been demonstrated to be effective with English language learners.

Lee, O., and S. Fradd. 1998. Science for all, including students from non-English-language backgrounds. *Educational Researcher* 27 (4): 12–21. A research paper describing the Instructional Congruence Model for structuring science teaching for English language learners.

Valdes, G. 2001. *Learning and not learning English: Latino students in American schools*. New York: Teachers College Press. Describes the lives, experiences, and struggle with learning English of four Mexican children in an American middle school.

One Teacher's Journey Toward Reformed Teaching

Sherry A. Southerland
Florida State University
Karen Rose
Rickards High School, Tallahassee, Florida
Margaret Blanchard
North Carolina State University

Karen, an energetic secondary science teacher in the southeastern United States, has always focused on student learning. Her current professional goal is to better incorporate the nature of science into her teaching. The nature of science is the set of underlying principles describing what science is and is not and the rules by which scientific knowledge is gained. For instance, the nature of scientific knowledge is tentative, based on empirical evidence, and situated in a historical and cultural context. These characteristics distinguish science from other ways of knowing, such as aesthetics or religion. Scientific knowledge is gained through gathered evidence on which explanations are based. These explanations are then presented to the scientific community for consideration. Knowledge about the nature of science is a central aspect of science understanding, is a characteristic of being scientifically literate, and is emphasized in the National Science Education Standards (NRC 1996).

Karen had her students read a newspaper article describing how snakes had entered a room in the Navajo Tribal Administration Building on the reservation. The Navajos were worried by the presence of the reptiles—understanding snakes to be the messengers of bad news. A medicine man was called in to rid the building of the messengers as the employees prayed and carried out other spiritual ceremonies. An animal control officer explained that because of drought the snakes entered the buildings for water and cooler conditions.

The following is an excerpt from the discussion of the article in Karen's classroom:

Karen: Is one explanation more right than the other?
Student: No.
Karen: Why not?
Student: 'Cause I don't know. They sayin' two different things.
Karen: What's the Navajo belief based on?
Student: They tryin' to give a message.
Karen: Yes, but what's it based on?
Student: Myth.
Karen: You think it's based on myth, legend, cultural stories that have been passed down?
Student: Yeah, yeah.
Karen: What do you think the explanation of the animal control person is based on?
Student: Background.
Student: Prior knowledge with the animals.
Karen: His knowledge with animals. She said it was because of his scientific background.
Student: One is more scientifically correct than the other one.
Karen: What did we say we need…?
Student: Evidence.
Karen: Evidence. Which one is more likely to have evidence to back it up?
Student: The animal control officer.
Karen: Do you think that one is just as right as the other?
Student: No.
Student: Yeah.
Karen: So when we look at the science of it, is one explanation more valid than the other?
Student: Yeah. Ours would be more valid.
Student: One's more logical.
Karen: Which one do you think is more logical?
Student: The one about them being hot and dry and needing water.
Student: Yeah.
Karen: All right, what's not logical about the fact that the snakes may be bringing a message?
Student: How can they bring a message? They ain't got no evidence that they bring a message….

Karen: OK. Now, let me ask you this, because now we're talking about Navajos, right? Your belief systems are different than theirs. But let's say that we were talking about whether or not you catch a cold if you go outside with your head wet. Let's say that your grandma's explanation is, yes, you catch a cold if you go outside with your hair wet.... The nurse comes along and says that's not why you have a cold. You have a cold because you were exposed to a virus. It made you sick.

Student: My grandma is right.

Karen: Why is it that now I am talking about your culture and your grandma, they are right, but the Navajos were not.

Student: They're superstitious.

Student: You might get a cold when you didn't go outside and someone might go outside with hair wet and be fine.

Karen: So, again, what you all are saying is now that I'm talking about your culture, the explanations are equally valid, but when I'm talking about somebody else's culture, they're superstitious and it's not valid because you don't have any evidence. Now, here I go, what evidence do you have that going outside with your head wet will give you a cold?

This discussion was characteristic of Karen's interactions with her students; she listened carefully and followed students' initial responses with questions encouraging elaboration. Karen also connected class material with students' past experiences. Are their grandmothers' cautions about covering a wet head different from the Navajos' belief that snakes are a warning? Karen wanted her students to wrestle with comparing the basis of different knowledge claims. In so doing, Karen's students could rethink their ideas in light of the new ones, take a stand, and make sense of new information in the context of their own experiences.

We believe that teachers like Karen are at the heart of school reform. Current reform efforts focus on scientific literacy for all students. To be scientifically literate is to understand the fundamental ideas of science, including how scientific knowledge is generated, so that it may be used to make informed personal and societal decisions. For teachers, inquiry-based teaching strategies support the learning of important science knowledge, as well as provide opportunities for students to experience knowledge construction (see Chapters 1 and 2 for additional details). This type of teaching, however, is different from what many of us have experienced as students. Therefore, teachers like Karen are central to reform. If science teaching is to change, teachers must change. Karen has accepted the challenge to change her teaching in order to improve student learning.

Since inquiry teaching in any of its forms (Abrams, Southerland, and Evans 2008) is not the norm of most university instruction, supporting changes of this type will largely occur in professional development settings. How did various professional development experiences help shape Karen as a teacher? Which experiences proved fruitful? And what might we take from Karen's experience as we explore ways to expand and further develop our teaching? This chapter chronicles a teacher's pursuit of learning about her classroom practice and provides one example of teacher change.

Karen's Teaching Path

Who is Karen? What drives her to experiment with her teaching? With a bachelor of science degree in biology, Karen pursued a teaching career because she was good with teenagers and found explaining things easy. She completed her student teaching in a large, urban school with a diverse student population. Here, she taught in ways similar to those experienced in her university methods courses and in her own learning as a student: She lectured, used questions from the book, and gave tests. Karen's first teaching position was in a seventh-grade science classroom in a large, urban school, where she was supported by a close-knit team of teachers. Teaching was a focus at this school, and teachers commonly talked about and shared ideas. Although the teachers periodically participated in one- or two-day inservice workshops, Karen did not view these experiences as particularly memorable. Karen explained, "These short-term inservices give you nice little strategies and things to use. But I don't really see them changing your teaching. I think what is needed to change your teaching are things that make you look at your classroom differently."

Three years later, a family move necessitated Karen's transfer to a much smaller, rural middle school with a large African American population and a large percentage of working class and working poor students. Karen was one of two science teachers, and her colleague was not interested in working collaboratively. This was unfortunate, as Karen was beginning to recognize that the traditional textbook, lecture, and test methods in use did not serve the student population well. Despite incremental improvements, after six years, Karen was feeling burned out. "There were some very bright students there," Karen emphasized, "but we were losing them—they were bored, they were dropping out." Karen left the school because she could not be as successful there as she wanted to be. She decided to move to a high school in the city. In this new position, Karen said, "I feel effective here, I feel as though I make a difference. I also believe I am a role model for the students. By bringing science *to* my students, I help them to see its relevance in their lives."

This story presents Karen as an individual who believes in herself as a teacher and in the capabilities of her students. Those beliefs acted as drivers for her to seek continual improvement as a teacher and to expect her students to achieve more in school. Leaving her former school was, in part, fueled by her confidence in her abilities and expectations to positively impact her students. This sense of high expectations of one's teaching is termed "teaching self-efficacy." Her discontentment with her former school and her own teaching approaches combined with her high personal expectations pushed Karen to seek additional professional development experiences. The short-term, activity-based experiences offered in her schools and district were not helping her better craft her teaching. Karen explained,

> *When I was working in this rural school, I found myself thinking "I know there has to be more." So I needed to find what I need to do to teach my students better. I always knew there was more and I wanted to try to learn more. And I also wanted to be able to pass on what I knew to other teachers…. [So I said to myself] "OK, it's time for me to go back to school, because if I am going to do this then I need to know how to teach other people better."*

Three Professional Development Experiences Dovetail

To improve her teaching, Karen sought professional development experiences that allowed her to better understand her own teaching and student learning. She found a number of experiences at her local university that were closely aligned in intent. Karen selected experiences that revolved around two central aspects of science education reform: inquiry and the nature of science. In this section, we'll describe how three such experiences interacted to help Karen refine her understanding of classroom inquiry.

Inquiry in a Graduate-Level Course

A graduate course in science teaching and learning introduced Karen to broader conceptions of inquiry and addressed conceptual change theory and the nature of science. Through a student interview assignment about a scientific topic, Karen was better able to uncover student thinking, including prior conceptions. She used this information to craft an instructional experience to help students change their science ideas. Through discussions in this course, Karen came to see science in ways that made sense, particularly as she thought about teaching. This view of science, however, was very different from her prior thinking about science. Karen's exposure to inquiry and the nature of science was at odds with other college experiences.

> *Even though I majored in biology, no one ever dealt with what is science and what it actually does, and the very nature of what science is. I used to think of science as the scientific method, and when the professor started describing aspects of the nature*

of science, I thought, "Well, OK. That's different. That's a new way to think about science." I mean, I thought you just wrote up your lab reports and that was it.

A Field-Based Research Experience

During the next summer, Karen participated in a five-week marine ecology program offered for teachers by the university. In it she learned about marine organisms and conducted scientific research. Karen was, in a sense, primed to examine her research experience because of the more theoretical lens she had developed in her graduate course. The scientific inquiry in the program was now informed by a more sophisticated understanding of learning and the nature of science. The experiences in the program emerged as an example of inquiry that could be used to shape her teaching.

The following school year, Karen introduced an inquiry-based lesson in which her high school students examined three different types of soil: peat moss, compost, and clay. Students were asked to record observations with a focus on color, texture, overall appearance, and any other observations other than tasting the soil, which she advised against. Using their observations, Karen helped her students craft questions about soil and turn them into experiments addressing the question, "How much water do these soils absorb?" As Karen reviewed the four-day unit with Meg (a doctoral student who was studying Karen's teaching as part of her dissertation research), they noted that Karen seemed reluctant to let students make mistakes in their experimental design. In one case, students wanted to use filter paper under their funnel. When Karen couldn't get the students to figure out where to place the filter, she finally told them where to place it.

A Structured Reflection on Classroom Inquiry

Following the analysis of Karen's inquiry-based teaching, Meg created a set of questions designed to uncover Karen's understanding of classroom inquiry and the basis of her instructional decision making. Meg explored Karen's reluctance to let her students pursue lab procedures that would not be productive. Karen told her,

> *When I first heard about inquiry it was years ago at a one-day workshop. It was the new thing and people around me were doing it…. I remember thinking that it was a ridiculous notion for me, because of the way it was described. The teachers just kind of "turned students loose" in the classroom, and the students were just supposed to discover these things on their own with no leadership from the teacher. I thought inquiry-based activities were supposed to be based only on the knowledge and experiences that the students already had. Toss the book out the door, and you let the kids go for it.*

Karen had difficulty making sense of this description of inquiry. Why would she not play a part in helping students learn? This residual memory affected Karen when she taught future inquiry lessons. Having students set up the soil labs in ways that were not correct or productive felt wasteful or somehow not reasonable to Karen. But she was willing to reconsider her attitude.

It wasn't until I took the graduate-level Science Teaching and Learning class that I saw inquiry as a continuum and got a better understanding of it. There is a continuum in there where you can work based on how you feel your students can handle [the experience] and make progress and so on and so forth. It then made more sense to me.

The Interactions of These Three Experiences

These three experiences were interwoven. Karen participated in a five-week research experience while she carried out inquiry-based activities prompted by the experience in her classroom. She resisted lesson elements that might make the activity more open-ended. In this case, she prevented her students from pursuing unproductive experimental designs. Although Karen had gained more holistic views of open-ended inquiry in her graduate course, she was still dealing with her

> **"Science education reform will not occur by simply adding occasional new activities to your teaching repertoire."**

initial negative impressions and feelings while simultaneously rethinking what inquiry meant in the context of her classroom. It was only as Karen worked to make sense of her many professional development experiences and the ways they were interrelated that she began to understand classroom inquiry more deeply, and she began to understand the various forms inquiry can take in a science classroom. She began to see that classroom inquiry requires a shift in responsibility for knowledge construction. After more than a year of exploring these issues, Karen continued to struggle with instructional methods that allowed her students to take more responsibility for their own learning.

What Kind of Professional Development Is Needed?

Karen's case reveals both good news and bad news about professional development and reform. The good news is that teachers can make low-risk changes in their teaching and evaluate the results. Karen's lesson described at the beginning of this chapter is such an example. This one-day activity required little in the way of planning, materials, or class time. The bad news: Science education reform will not occur by simply adding occasional new activities to your teaching repertoire. Reform requires thought, work, and persistence. Karen explains:

[Short-term inservice sessions] give you nice little strategies and things to use. But...I don't see them really changing your teaching.... I think what is needed to change your teaching are things that make you look at your classroom differently. **Teachers need ... not new things to do, but new ways to see their classrooms.** [Boldface added for emphasis.]

Reform requires us to rethink our teaching, to view teaching through different eyes. Such change requires professional development experiences that are long term and sustained. The experiences must challenge teachers to consider new ways of thinking about teaching, as opposed to merely providing them with new activities. As Karen elaborated,

You have to have time to digest these ideas, to think about them. You can't just read an article, then produce some new [instructional] product. You have to think about your teaching, your students, and all that takes time. If you're just given new activities to do, then you're pretty much just doing the same thing. You are just changing the things that you do. **You're not changing the way you perceive the class and how it should and can go.** [Boldface added for emphasis.]

For Karen, what made the difference was participating in a variety of professional development experiences that focused on her *own* teaching. This mixture of graduate classes, research experiences, and reflections was essential in providing Karen with an extended opportunity to consider her classroom. As part of these experiences, Karen developed a network of colleagues who provided support as she attempted to rethink her teaching practice. These experiences are similar to those suggested in Chapter 2.

Karen's case allows us to see that there is no secret recipe for professional development (e.g., take a graduate class, followed by a research experience, topped off by a year of dissertation research in your classroom). Instead, it is important to recognize that reform takes time. It takes sustained effort. It takes the goal of better understanding your classrooms and your teaching. Profound professional development starts from and ends in experiences that are applicable to the classroom.

For Karen, analysis of learning theory—combined with seeing the ways learning theory played out in classrooms—caused her to think about teaching in new ways. Professional development does not need to follow the path Karen took, however. A well-selected series of workshops, virtual courses, or attendance at science teacher conferences can allow for similar shifts in our teaching. A long-term book group with teaching colleagues can also be transformative. Additional ideas for transformative professional development opportunities can be found in Loucks-Horsley et al. (2003). The learning opportunities you select are less important than recognizing that crafting your own circuitous route to reform takes time and sustained effort. Your goal must be to better understand your teaching.

What Kind of Teachers Seek to Reform Their Practice?

Most science teachers know that what a student learns depends on what that student already knows and how willing that student is to engage with a new idea. Teachers are no different. Karen's case demonstrates how her learning from a professional development experience was influenced by her prior knowledge and degree of engagement with the material. Karen's learning in the research experience was shaped by her own evolving knowledge of learning theory, conceptual change, and classroom inquiry. This knowledge allowed for Karen's deep engagement with the material, an engagement fostered by a five-week intensive research experience and the availability of someone (Meg) to help her make sense of her teaching. This knowledge and deep engagement—the willingness to continue working and refining until she was pleased with the result—allowed Karen to learn more from her experiences than other teachers who were more superficially involved in courses and professional development.

Karen's story also allows us to see how a teacher's sense of self shapes learning. Karen held high expectations for her students and high teaching self-efficacy. She expected to teach effectively. These characteristics were combined with a sense of discontentment with her teaching. Although Karen knew she was able to teach well, she recognized that she did not always teach well. Indeed, Karen recognized that not all students were learning as well as she expected, a responsibility she reflected back onto her teaching. High teaching self-efficacy combined with teaching discontentment made Karen a prime candidate for learning from sustained professional development. If Karen didn't have high expectations of herself and of her students, she may not have attempted the new ideas presented in professional development. Alternatively, if she thought she *was* already teaching as effectively as possible, she probably would not have seen the value in applying the ideas presented in the professional development.

Implications for Teachers, Professional Developers, and Policy Makers

Karen's case clarifies several points about professional development:

* No single professional development experience is sufficient to produce change in a teacher's understanding or a teacher's practice. For this reason, teachers need a variety of professional development experiences to support them in their progress toward reform-based science teaching.

* The effectiveness of professional development experiences will vary as a result of a teacher's emotional readiness to learn from such an experience. For optimal learning to occur, teachers must believe that they can teach well and yet be unsatisfied with some aspect of their teaching. As a result, not all teachers will learn to the same degree as a result of a professional development experience. Forcing teachers to participate in unwanted professional development experiences may not be an effective use of limited time and resources. Instead, teachers need support to engage in experiences they recognize as potentially useful.

* The effectiveness of a professional development experience will depend on the cognitive readiness of the teacher to learn from the experience. Professional developers and policy makers must carefully consider the optimal sequencing of experiences to impact teachers' learning.

* Finally, reform-based teaching practices take a great deal of time and effort. There are no quick fixes. As Karen reminds us:

Teachers have to have time to digest these ideas, to think about them. You can't just read an article, then produce some new [instructional] product. You have to think about your teaching, your students, and all that takes time.

Recommended Resources

Abrams, E., S. A. Southerland, and C. Evans. 2008. An introduction to inquiry. In *Inquiry in the classroom: Realities and opportunities,* eds. E. Abrams, S. A. Southerland, and P. Silva, pp. i–xiii. Greenwich, CT: Information Age Publishing. Discusses the various forms inquiry can take in the science classroom and provides teachers with a way of thinking about the form of inquiry that may be most appropriate for their particular classrooms.

Hammrich, P. L., and K. K. Blouch. 1998. A cooperative controversy lesson designed to reveal students' conceptions of the "nature of science." *American Biology Teacher* 60 (1): 50–51. Looks at "cooperative controversy," an instructional strategy that examines students' conceptions of the nature of science by presenting situations in which one person's ideas, information, conclusions, theories, or opinions are incompatible with those of another.

Horner, J. K., and P. Rubba. 1978. The myth of absolute truth. *Science Teacher* 45 (1): 29–30. Discusses the nature of science and addresses the question of why scientific knowledge cannot be absolute.

Loucks-Horsley, S., N. Love, K. Stiles, S. Mundry, and P. Hewson. 2003. Designing professional development for teachers of science and mathematics. 2nd ed. Thousand Oaks, CA: Corwin Press. Discusses the important interaction of content, context, and design needed for effective mathematics and science teacher professional development.

McComas, W. F. 1996. Ten myths of science: Reexamining what we think we know. *School Science and Mathematics* 96 (1): 10–16. Describes students' and teachers' common misconceptions regarding the nature of science.

Michaels, E., and R. L. Bell. 2003. The nature of science and perceptual frameworks. *The Science Teacher* 70 (8): 36–39. Provides an analysis of the tentative nature of science and portrays science as a dynamic and human endeavor. Includes a discussion about how such topics can be addressed in the classroom.

Nott, M., and J. Wellington. 1995. Critical incidents in the science classroom and the nature of science. *School Science Review* 76 (276): 41–46. Provides examples of critical incidents that can promote discussion and reflection on the nature of science. Discusses teachers' views on critical evaluation of practical work, reliability, and replicability of experiments, accepted scientific explanations, scientific evidence, religious beliefs, and moral dilemmas.

Smith, M. U., and L. C. Scharmann. 1998. Defining versus describing the nature of science: A pragmatic analysis for classroom teachers and science educators. *Science Education* 83 (4): 493–509. Provides a useful discussion of the central components of the nature of science as well as practical advice for how these ideas can be addressed in a classroom.

References

Abrams, E., S. A. Southerland, and C. Evans. 2008. An introduction to inquiry. In *Inquiry in the classroom: Realities and opportunities,* eds. E. Abrams, S. A. Southerland, and P. Silva, pp. i–xiii. Greenwich, CT: Information Age Publishing.

American Association for the Advancement of Science (AAAS). 1990. *Project 2061: Science for all Americans.* New York: Oxford University Press. Available from *www.project2061.org/publications/sfaa/online/sfaatoc.htm*

American Association for the Advancement of Science (AAAS). 1993. *Benchmarks for science literacy.* New York: Oxford University Press. Available from *www.project2061.org/publications/bsl/online*

American Association for the Advancement of Science (AAAS). 2001. *Atlas of science literacy.* Washington, DC: AAAS and the National Science Teachers Association. Sample maps only available from *www.project2061.org/publications/atlas/sample/toc.htm*

Ball, D. L., and D. K. Cohen. 1996. Reform by the book: What is—or might be—the role of curriculum materials in teacher learning and instructional reform? *Educational Researcher* 25 (9): 6–8, 14.

Bell, J. A., and A. Buccino. 1997. *Seizing opportunities: Collaborating for excellence in teacher preparation.* Washington, DC: American Association for the Advancement of Science.

Ben-Peretz, M. 1990. *The teacher-curriculum encounter: Freeing teachers from the tyranny of texts.* Albany, NY: State University of New York Press.

Bransford, J. D., A. L. Brown, and R. R. Cocking, eds. 2000. *How people learn: Brain, mind, experience, and school.* Washington, DC: National Academy Press. Available from *www.nap.edu/catalog.php?record_id=9853#toc*

Brearton, M. A., and S. Shuttleworth. 1999. Racing a comet. *Journal of Staff Development* (winter): 30–33. Retrieved from *http://project2061.aaas.org/newsinfo/research/articles/nsdc_jsd.htm*

Brown, M., and D. D. Edelson. 2003. *Teaching as design: Can we better understand the ways in which teachers use materials so we can better design materials to support their changes in practice?* Evanston, IL: Design Brief Center for Learning Technologies in Urban Schools.

Bullough, R., J. Birrell, J. Young, C. Clark, L. Erickson, R. Earle, J. Campbell, L. Hansen, and M. Egan. 1999. Paradise unrealized: Teacher educators and the costs and benefits of school/university partnerships. *Journal of Teacher Education* 50 (5): 381–390.

Committee on Prospering in the Global Economy of the 21st Century. 2006. *Rising above the gathering storm: Energizing and employing America for a brighter economic future.* Retrieved from National Academies Press *www.nap.edu/catalog/11463.html*

Costa, A. L., and R. J. Garmston. 2002. *Cognitive coaching: A foundation for renaissance schools.* Norwood, MA: Christopher-Gordon Publishers.

Davis, E. A., and J. Krajcik. 2005. Designing educative curriculum materials to promote teacher learning. *Educational Researcher* 34 (3): 3–14.

Donovan, M. S., and J. D. Bransford, eds. 2005. *How students learn: Science in the classroom.* Washington, DC: National Academy Press.

Driver, R., A. Squires, P. Rushworth, and V. Wood-Robinson. 1994. *Making sense of secondary science: Research into children's ideas.* New York: Routledge Press.

DuFour, R., and R. Eaker. 1998. *Professional learning communities at work: Best practices for enhancing student achievement.* Bloomington, IN: National Education Service.

Education Development Center, Inc. (EDC). 2001. *Implementation fidelity: Investigating how teachers use innovative curriculum in the classroom.* Final Report Small Grants for Exploratory Research. Newton, MA: EDC.

Eisenkraft, A. 2000. *Active physics.* Armonk, NY: It's About Time Publishing.

Eisenkraft, A., and G. Freebury. 2003. *Active chemistry.* Armonk, NY: It's About Time Publishing.

Friedman, T. L. 2005. *The world is flat: A brief history of the twenty-first century.* New York: Farrar, Straus, and Giroux.

Fullan, M. 2001. *The new meaning of educational change.* 3rd ed. New York: Teachers College Press.

Garcia, E. 2002. *Student cultural diversity: Understanding and meeting the challenge.* 3rd ed. Boston: Houghton Mifflin.

Garmston, R. J., and B. M. Wellman. 1999. *The adaptive school: A sourcebook for developing and facilitating collaborative groups.* Norwood, MA: Christopher-Gordon Publishers.

Gibbons, B. A. 2003. Supporting elementary science education for English learners: A constructivist evaluation instrument. *Journal of Educational Research* 96 (6): 371–380.

Hall, G. E., and S. M. Hord. 2001. *Implementing change: Patterns, principles, and potholes.* Needham Heights, MA: Allyn and Bacon.

Harvey, T. R. 1995. *Checklist for change: A pragmatic approach to creating and controlling change.* Lancaster, PA: Technomic Publishing.

Harvey, T. R., and B. Drolet. 1994. *Building teams, building people: Expanding the fifth resource.* Lancaster, PA: Technomic Publishing Company.

Johnson, C. C., J. B. Kahle, and J. Fargo. 2007 Effective teaching results in increased science achievement for all students. *Science Education* 91 (3): 371–383.

Keeley, P. 2005. *Science curriculum topic study.* Thousand Oaks, CA: Corwin Press.

Lambert, L. 2003. *Leadership capacity for lasting school improvement.* Alexandria, VA: Association for Supervision and Curriculum Development.

Lee, O. 2004. Teacher change in beliefs and practices in science and literacy instruction with English Language Learners. *Journal of Research in Science Teaching* 41 (1): 65–93.

Lee, O., and S. H. Fradd. 2001. Instructional congruence to promote science learning and literacy development for linguistically diverse students. In *Models of science teacher preparation*, eds. D. R. Lavoie and W. M. Roth, 109–126. Dordrecht: The Netherlands: Kluwer Academic Publishers.

Loucks-Horsley, S., N. Love, K. Stiles, S. Mundry, and P. Hewson. 2003. *Designing professional development for teachers of science and mathematics.* 2nd ed. Thousand Oaks, CA: Corwin Press.

Louis, K. S., and S. D. Kruse. 1995. *Professionalism and community: Perspectives on reforming urban schools.* Thousand Oaks, CA: Corwin Press.

Love, N. 2002. *Using data/getting results: A practical guide to school improvement in mathematics and science.* Norwood, MA: Christopher-Gordon Publishers.

Miles, M. 1998. Finding keys to school change: A 40 year odyssey. *International Handbook of Educational Change*, eds. A. Hargeaves, A. Lieberman, M. Fullan, and D. Hopkins, 37–69. Dordrecht: The Netherlands: Kluwer Academic Publishers.

National Center for Education Statistics (NCES). 2003. The condition of education 2003 in brief. U.S. Department of Education, Institute of Education Sciences. Retrieved from *http://nces.ed.gov/pubs2003/2003068.pdf*

National Commission on Excellence in Education (NCEE). 1983. *A nation at risk.* Retrieved from *www.ed.gov/pubs/NatAtRisk/index.html*

National Research Council (NRC). 1996. *National science education standards.* Retrieved from National Academies Press *www.nap.edu/catalog.php?record_id=4962#toc*

National Research Council (NRC). 2000. *Inquiry and the national science education standards: A guide for teaching and learning.* Washington, DC: National Academy Press.

Powell, J., J. Short, and N. Landes. 2002. Curriculum reform, professional development, and powerful learning. In *Learning science and the science of learning*, ed. R. Bybee, 121–136. Arlington, VA: NSTA Press.

Richardson, J. 2005. Transform your group into a team. *Tools for Schools* 9 (2): 1–7.

Rutherford, F. J. 2000. Coherence in high school science. In *Making sense of integrated science: A guide for high schools*. Colorado Springs, CO: BSCS.

Schmidt, W. H., C. C. McKnight, R. T. Houang, H. C. Wang, D. E. Wiley, L. S. Cogan, and G. Wolfe. 2001. *Why schools matter: A cross-national comparison of curriculum and learning*. San Francisco: Jossey-Bass.

Senge, P. M., C. Roberts, R. B. Ross, B. J. Smith, and A. Kleiner. 1994. *The fifth discipline fieldbook*. New York: Doubleday.

Sirotnik, K. A., and J. Goodlad, eds. 1988. *School-university partnerships in action: Concepts, cases, and concerns*. New York: Teachers College Press.

Smedley, L. 2001. Impediments to partnerships: A literature review of school-university links. *Teaching and Teachers: Theory and Practice* 7 (2): 189–221.

Taylor, J., J. Powell, K. Bess, and T. Lamb. 2005. Examining the professional growth of out-of-field physics teachers: Findings from a pilot study. *Journal of Physics Teacher Education Online* 2 (4): 16–22.

Thompson, C. L., and J. S. Zeuli. 1999. The frame and the tapestry. In *Teaching as the learning profession: Handbook of policy and practice,* eds. L. Darling-Hammond and G. Sykes, 341–375. San Francisco: Jossey-Bass.

Tuckman, B. 1965. Developmental sequence in small groups. *Psychological Bulletin* 63: 384–399.

About the Authors

Jeffrey Arnold is the director of the Teacher/Leader Quality Partnership Program, Daemen College, in Amherst, New York.

Randy L. Bell is an associate professor at the Curry School of Education, University of Virginia, in Charolottesville, Virginia.

Jody Bintz is a science educator in the Center for Professional Development at BSCS, in Colorado Springs, Colorado.

Margaret Blanchard is an assistant professor of science education at North Carolina State University, in Raleigh, North Carolina.

Rodger W. Bybee is executive director emeritus at BSCS, in Colorado Springs, Colorado.

Joëlle Clark is a professional development coordinator in the Department of Anthropology at Northern Arizona University, in Flagstaff, Arizona.

April L. Gardner is a senior researcher in the Center for Research and Evaluation at BSCS, in Colorado Springs, Colorado.

Julie Gess-Newsome is the J. Lawrence Walkup distinguished professor and director of the Center for Science Teaching and Learning at Northern Arizona University, in Flagstaff, Arizona.

Carla C. Johnson is an associate professor of science education at the University of Cincinnati, in Cincinnati, Ohio.

Ruth Krumhansl is a senior curriculum design associate in the Center for Science Education at Education Development Center, Inc., in Newton, Massachusetts.

Nancy Landes is the director of the Center for Professional Development at BSCS, in Colorado Springs, Colorado.

Xiufeng Liu is an associate professor in the Department of Learning and Instruction, State University of New York at Buffalo, in Buffalo, New York.

Julie A. Luft is a professor of science education at Mary Lou Felton College of Education at the Arizona State University, in Tempe, Arizona.

Lee Meadows is an associate professor in the Schools of Education and Medicine at the University of Alabama at Birmingham, in Birmingham, Alabama.

Jackie Mensaco is the associate director of professional development in the Center for Science Teaching and Learning at Northern Arizona University, in Flagstaff, Arizona.

Jacqueline S. Miller is a senior research scientist in the Center for Science Education at Education Development Center, Inc., in Newton, Massachusetts.

Karen Rose is a high school biology teacher at Rickards High School, in Tallahassee, Florida. Following the experiences described in Chapter 9, she achieved National Board Certification.

Sherry A. Southerland is an associate professor of science education in the School of Teacher Education at Florida State University, in Tallahassee, Florida.

Joseph A. Taylor is the director of the Center for Research and Evaluation at BSCS, in Colorado Springs, Colorado.

Joseph Zawicki is an assistant professor in the Department of Earth Science and Science Education at State University of New York at Buffalo, in Buffalo, New York.

Index

*Page numbers in **boldface** type refer to tables or figures.*

teachers' use of, 43–44

The Teacher–Curriculum Encounter: Freeing Teachers From the Tyranny of Texts, 44

Thompson, J. J., 7

Time frame for change, 19, 21

Transformative professional development, 110–111

    Analyzing Instructional Materials process for, 35–36

Tuckman, B., 60

V

Visual representations of concepts, 100–101

W

Wellman, B. M., 54, 57, 58

WestEd, 32, 54

Writing in science, 100